MW01615037

FIRST CATCH YOUR
RABBIT!
OR COOKING WITHOUT FEAR

SIMON MAHONEY

Copyright © 2020 by Simon Mahoney
Published by Aye Aye Publishing

Website: www.WingingItBlind.com

All rights reserved. No part of this book may
be reproduced or transmitted in any form
or by any means, electronic or mechanical,
including photocopying or recording without
the permission of the author.

Cover design and layout
by www.spiffingcovers.com

Paperback ISBN-13: 978-1-9164463-3-5
.epub eBook ISBN-13: 978-1-9164463-4-2
.mobi eBook ISBN-13: 978-1-9164463-5-9

First Catch Your Rabbit, for my Australian cousins and Doug the Doubtful.

And in loving memory of Kelly, my lover, best friend and wife,

30.9.1943 to 20.3.2020.

ACKNOWLEDGEMENTS

My thanks to Fiona and Denise for brutally transforming my kitchen.

To Dury, my grandson, for being bold enough to try the food and for filming.

To Maggie, Sylvia, Mo, Lorna and Graham for their constant encouragement.

To Jae, Kuffy, Cary, Louie and Doug for contributions.

To Polly and Will specifically from Blind Veterans UK for their unstinting efforts on my behalf.

To Blind Veterans UK generally for their support and consistent efforts on behalf of the project.

To the team at Spiffing Covers – Gabriel,

Kimberley, James and Richard – for their professionalism and work on the book to transform it into a silk purse.

Finally, my thanks to OTW, ITCRM (Officer Training Wing, Infantry Training Centre Royal Marines) for providing an excruciating character-forming experience which has been instrumental in overcoming the challenges of my sight loss.

Note: No rabbit was harmed or even alarmed whilst writing this book.

TABLE OF CONTENTS

FOREWORD

Well, what can I say?

This man never ceases to amaze me. Not only with coping with his sight loss but with many aspects of his life. How many blind people do you know who have walked along Hadrian's Wall, ridden on the back of a bike in a velodrome, flown an aircraft and sailed many times on Carsington Water?

I first met Simon about six years ago when I started cleaning for him and his wife Kelly. Over this six-year period I became more than just a cleaner, but a friend too.

Sadly, last March, Simon's wife died. Not only was Kelly Simon's wife, she was also his eyes. Simon mourned his wife's passing, but he mourned the loss of his sight all over again too.

Kelly did most of the cooking, and now that she was gone Simon had to learn to cook. We set to and reorganised his kitchen, and tailored it just for him. It had to be precise. Anything dangerous was removed, and all the cupboards were sorted through and rearranged until everything was in reach of Simon's work station where he prepared all his meals. To help us do this, Simon had a special pen that allowed us to label all the food. This meant he had to open only one jar or tin instead of half a dozen to find what he was looking for!

On one occasion when I was there, Simon was busy in the kitchen. Later he presented me with a piece of pie, and I asked him if he had made it. He said yes. I then asked what was in it, and he replied that it was apple, onion, walnut and stilton savoury pie. I couldn't believe he had made it himself! It was delicious!

This book is not just for people with sight loss. My daughter, who has dyslexia and is just learning to cook, found the book very easy to follow. Therefore, this book is for anybody who thinks they'll never learn to cook at all, or wants to cook again if they have stopped.

From the simple idea of showing **how** rather than **what** to cook, *First Catch Your Rabbit* was born.

Denise Ball

PREFACE

I was trying to cook something, I don't remember what – back in the early stages of bumbling around my kitchen without my wife, trying not to fall over the dogs and the cat and a danger to myself (and them) – when it occurred to me that I needed to develop some sort of system to avoid damaging or killing myself in the process. The phrase 'First catch your rabbit' popped into my head, which is something my mum used to misquote, as it is a play on the proverb 'First catch your hare', which in simple terms means don't plan what you will do with something until you actually have it; or in other words, get your ducks in a row before you start a thing!

It occurred to me that had I first caught my rabbit, or lined my ducks up, I wouldn't still be bumbling around my kitchen, not sure where anything was or how to cook even the most basic food without danger to life!

The next thing that happened was I imagined a book cover – this book cover – and it made me laugh, as it felt very much like the rabbit had caught me! Then came the realisation: *I might have to write the thing now.*

I couldn't help thinking about how many people might benefit from a cookbook like this, as well as the blind or partially sighted: kids who want to learn to cook; students with no cooking skills; young mums with not much time to cook (or who have never been taught); widowers whose wives did all the cooking; people genuinely fearful of the kitchen; those with various types of special needs. The list went on. And then came the second realisation: *Oh dear, I'm definitely going to have to write the thing now!*

So here it is.

INTRODUCTION

'Cooking is a game you can eat.'

– Louie Foreman, 2020

Many people with sight impairment refuse to even consider cooking:

- Too complicated!
- Too dangerous!
- No idea what you are touching!
- Impossible!

I have heard it all. Interestingly, I was talking to a sighted person about this and they were quite clear that if they lost their sight there was no way they would consider continuing cooking.

I contend that anyone can prepare food and feed themselves successfully. I am completely blind and do it every day. What is required, above all else, is a positive attitude, a belief that you can do it, and a willingness to do the work.

What I am talking about is wholesome scran[1] that will sustain and keep you healthy. If you wish to go on to more sophisticated gourmet food after you have mastered the basics, good luck to you. I do occasionally just for the craic![2]

This is not a cook book in the regular sense. Every day I cook meals for myself and sometimes for other people too. People kept saying how amazing it was that I could prepare and cook food without killing myself in the process. As far as I am concerned, I was just responding to a necessity and could see nothing amazing in it.

The result of all those comments, however, is this book. It is a book about how to survive in the kitchen when you cannot see. It is all logical, simple and, more to the point, doable. As such, it may also be useful for someone who has never cooked before, whether they can see or not.

The book deals with the very basics

---

1. Forces slang for 'food'!
2. Slang for 'just for fun/just for the hell of it'.

and there is a presumption of absolutely no cooking knowledge whatsoever.

From this it follows that a lot of space is given to safety, organisation, equipment, implements and basic foods you need to have in stock. Various techniques are demonstrated through the different recipes, which are graded in difficulty.

The emphasis will, throughout the book, be on safety and organisation. As a person with sight impairment, or even without, these are the key to seamless, basic food preparation and cooking.

Whether we like it or not, we have to take our sight loss into consideration. This means that any skills acquisition has to be in baby steps. When you have sight loss it is not too clever if you try to run before you know the exact whereabouts of the ground!

It is accepted that those of us with sight loss, or our clothes, are not generally fans of the knife and fork. For reasons I have yet to fathom I just can't master them. I therefore tend to cook food that can be eaten with just a fork. (Anything that needs to be cut up is dealt with at the cooking stage.) I also tend to go for quite a lot of finger food. In addition to this, I use a high-sided plate or bowl so I can trap the food against the sides.

I have one of these at my local pub and they call it 'Simon's dog bowl'. This invariably horrifies new members of staff and vexes the hell out of environmental health! If you look for enamel pie dishes, these are perfect. It's simply a case of accepting things as they are and certainly nothing to be upset about. It is just one of the many adaptations I have made since becoming blind.

It is important to appreciate that I am explaining how I cook, the food is to my taste, that the information is a heads up to get you cooking. Mine is not the only way and my food is not to every one's taste. The contents of this book are for your guidance and not your direction.

Simon Mahoney
Ashbourne, 2020

BASIC RULES FOR THE KITCHEN

- Keep it simple.
- Remain focussed at all times.
- Move about as little as possible.
- Reverse engineer every meal (this will be explained).
- Keep everything within reach.
- Remove all clutter and items not in use.
- Have the sequence of events clear in your head before starting any recipe or task.
- Finish a task before starting the next.
- Clear any mess out of the work tray as you go.
- Wash and dry hands frequently.

There are hot tips with every recipe about how to stay safe and organised, and some about the food or methods.

THE SLOPE PRINCIPLE

'What we're talking about here, is cooking without fear.'

– Dr Cary Sadler, 2020,
walking doctor and friend

Do not skip this part. All of it is important. And if you think it isn't, try cleaning up after beating three eggs in a colander!

When one part of you does not work, this places a strain on the rest. It is therefore important that what we eat is of good quality. The cheapest and most effective way to achieve this is to **cook meals from scratch with fresh ingredients.** (If you choose to use ready meals they must be of good quality.)

At this level, or indeed any level, there

is one **overriding principle** to preparing and cooking food: **KISS:**

Keep
It
Simple
Stupid

As a general principle this makes absolute sense, as preparing food can be tricky enough without looking for complications! If you have a sight impairment, life is even more so, so we want to avoid creating further problems.

The answer? Keep things as simple and straight forward as possible.

The best way to do this is to break the task down into simple bite-sized components. This brings in the **five aspects of food preparation and cooking**. It cannot be stressed enough that each part is important. Indeed, leave any one of them out and you risk the success of the whole process. The five aspects form the acronym **SLOPE:**

Safety
Lazy person principle
Organisation
Preparation
Execution

Safety

The kitchen is the most dangerous place in the house. There is a combination of electricity, water, hot surfaces and boiling water, sharp objects, trip hazards and open cupboard doors. Add to this not being able to see, and you have a potential health and safety nightmare. For this reason, safety must always be in the front of your mind when working in the kitchen. Try and anticipate hazards and either remove or lessen them.

The single most important thing we need to understand is that when we were sighted we did things blindly. Now that we are blind that is no longer an option, and we must do things mindfully. Understanding this one thing will cut out the majority of accidents.

Lazy person principle

This is based on the premise that you are not a lazy person personally, but must move with the slow, minimal movements of a lazy person. If you are blind, every movement holds the potential for an accident. Therefore, as a person with sight impairment we must keep our movements to a minimum. This does not mean that you freeze like a startled rabbit, but rather that you do not make unnecessary movements. This is a follow on from the safety aspect, and should influence how you go about organising the kitchen in general, and your food preparation in particular.

Further to this, if you remain still there is a greater chance of focussing on the job rather than thinking about other things. The very idea of tottering about, preoccupied, with hot saucepans or dishes of food that have been in the oven when you cannot see is the stuff of nightmares, and has only one result: tears before bedtime!

The story of the old bull and the young bull also reminds us that sometimes we achieve more by taking it steady.

Organisation

This means the long-term organisation of your kitchen not just a short-term tidy-up. For example:

- I have put my general waste and recycling bins in a cupboard so that they do not restrict the floor space and present a trip hazard.
- I have created a specific work area for food preparation. It is within reach of the sink, the basic food cupboards, power points and the one-cup kettle.
- A tray is permanently placed on the worktop and all implements, knives and chopping boards are within reach. This way I know exactly where everything is and can focus on the work in hand.

In other words, my kitchen is permanently arranged according to the lazy person principle. I only have to slide along the worktop to access the standing equipment such as the microwave, oven and hob.

I am not a fan of leaning across hot front rings in order to access the back ones, so the hob has been reduced to two rings (the back ones have been disabled). In addition to this, I had a low rail fitted on the worktop in front of the hob. This prevents me from touching the hot hob and also stops saucepans from being knocked onto the floor. Having done it once, I have no desire for a repetition!

My other equipment has been reduced to a minimum to include an electric wok, toaster, sandwich maker, frying pan and slow cooker. And I have reduced my pans to just three different sized saucepans (with lids) and a wok.

With respect to timing the cooking, I have a talking watch. But Alexa will do the job equally as well, as will Siri or similar timing app on your smartphone.

All the electrical equipment has knobs and switches rather than buttons, and are analogue not digital – except the talking microwave, which is digital. All equipment has been selected for ease of operation, un-breakability and simplicity; and aside from two ovenproof dishes, all bowls, containers and baking trays are either plastic or metal.

Similarly, implements have been reduced to a minimum and are either wood or plastic. Knives have been selected for their grip and sharpness, and have also been reduced to the minimum.

When organising a specific meal, the first action is to **reverse engineer it**. In other words, think about the finished meal and identify all the ingredients and equipment you will need and ensure that they are available, fit for purpose, and clean. This reverse engineering process must be carried out for each meal. You may find this tedious, and it is, but it is important, because it prevents you rushing about trying to locate food or equipment whilst preparing the meal. Rushing about is when many accidents happen. Indeed, it could be argued that in the kitchen you are only one wrong step away from visiting the local Accident and Emergency Department!

Preparation

This is where you set everything up for preparing the meal. If you do it right, you will not have to move during the food preparation phase until it is time to put the result of your efforts into the oven.

This, from much experience, is what works really well:

- Ensure the work tray is in place at the work station.
- Put ingredients in the tray.
- Place implements to one side of the tray and equipment on the other.
- Have a large empty bowl handy for any rubbish. This prevents going backwards and forwards to the waste bin when working, and mixing the rubbish up with the food you will be cooking.
- Make sure there is a bowl of hot soapy water available in the sink or close by with a clean towel (and away from the food).
- Finally, make sure the worktop is clear of everything that you are not going to use.

Following these guidelines, every time, keeps things as simple as possible, but is based on how my kitchen is set out. Yours will most likely be slightly different, in which case you may have to arrange things to suit you. This is not important provided you end up with a layout and system that works for you. But whatever adjustments you make, every effort should be made to keep the working area as uncluttered as possible. The use of the work tray is the key.

Execution

This is the part of the whole process where you have to concentrate on what you are doing *all the time*, and provided you have got your organisation and preparation right, this should be a very simple matter of preparing the food and following the cooking instructions. This is why everything has led to you being anchored in one place so you can focus. An important technique here is visualisation.

Visualisation is where you follow what you are doing in your mind's eye. This makes it easier and is a good way to record and keep track of what you have done. This technique is not a substitute for seeing, however, but rather a way of adding to what your hands are telling you. Be warned that after a prolonged period of visualisation, it can be quite shocking when you come out of it and realise that you are blind. I do this all the time!

Another basic technique is using a knife safely:

- First of all, the knife must be sharp. A blunt one means you have to apply more force and that causes accidents.
- When chopping or slicing, slowly bring the knife in contact with the side of your forefinger. This way you provide a guide for the knife and, more importantly, you know the whereabouts of the sharp side!
- Where possible, cut away from yourself. This prevents you stabbing yourself if the knife slips.
- When not in use, the knife should be laid down next to the work tray with the handle towards you.

There are also certain habits you have to develop:

- Shut cupboard doors and drawers or they will trip you or smack you in the head.
- Turn pan handles parallel with the worktop. If they are overhanging and

you tip boiling water on yourself it will ruin your day and your meal!

- Keep things as tidy as possible as you go along.
- Never rush. Blindness plus rushing equals chaos; and chaos equals accidents.
- Wash and dry your hands frequently.
- Put lids back on jars immediately after use and only open one jar at a time.
- Listen for sizzling butter or boiling water to let you know when it's ready for cooking.
- Your sense of smell will quickly recognise when food is cooked, or burnt, which you'll learn to avoid if you don't like the taste of carbon!

The most important thing is to stay aware and mindful at all times, and stop and take a breath and gather your thoughts (and yourself) if you need to. With practice, your confidence will grow and you'll be amazed at what you can achieve.

If I had

When you are standing in your kitchen full of hubris and thinking 'I've nailed this,' something invariably happens to cut you down to size.

We had got to the stage where we were discussing the final edited draft, my editor and I, and she had given me much to think about. After our conversation ended I set about making a quiche, and I did something that was so staggeringly stupid that it beggars belief.

If I had followed the drill;
If I had reverse engineered the meal;
If I had worked within the tray;
If I had remained focussed;
If I had double-checked!

Then it would never have happened.

I grabbed a bowl out of the cupboard. I cracked three eggs into it and added herbs and salt and pepper. I then proceeded to beat the mixture ready for the quiche.

It took a few seconds before the penny dropped: the strange, hollow rattling noise told me, and everyone else, that I was trying to beat eggs in a colander!

If you have skipped the preceding part, I suggest you go back and reread or listen to it again now!

Basic food stocks

If you are going to prepare food on a regular basis you will need a stock of basic food, flavourings and condiments. Again, this is based on what I feel are the bare necessities. You, of course, are free to choose others.

I always keep: potatoes, tomatoes, onions, peppers, mushrooms, long grain rice, dried pasta (macaroni, fusilli, penne, tagliatelle and shells), oats, eggs, milk, plain flour, grated cheese, lazy garlic, chopped chili, lazy ginger, salt and pepper, curry paste, oil, butter or spread, and tinned goods such as chopped tomatoes, baked beans, pilchards or tuna, and sweetcorn.

In addition to this, I also keep frozen peas, frozen peppers, frozen sweetcorn, frozen chopped onion and frozen grated cheese as part of my basics.

I always make sure I have a range of herbs too, namely basil, thyme, chives, mint and rosemary. The beauty of these particular herbs is that they all smell and feel different and are easy to identify.

It sounds like quite a lot of stuff, but there is less than thirty pounds-worth here, and provided you keep it maintained and topped up it will give you the ability to ring the changes on your cooking.

All the above, except for the peppers, mushrooms and milk, have a good shelf life. Mushrooms have to be checked daily. Peppers should last a week, and milk should not be used beyond the use-by date. (If in doubt, sniff it!)

It is important that you put labels on your food. I use an electronic pen friend, which enables me to put an audio label on whatever I want.

I also convert the adhesive labels that are supplied on food into transferable labels by mounting them on a piece of plastic with a rubber band attached. That way I can use them repeatedly instead of just once. The data I record is what the item is and the use-by date.

If you are blind, an electronic pen friend is an extremely important bit of kit, but you will not see much change out of a hundred pounds. It may be time to badger friends or relatives! Talk to Blind Veterans UK or the RNIB (Royal National Institute of Blind People) and they will be able to advise on this.

Note: Don't drop your electronic pen friend in water. They don't like it!

Notes on ovens

All ovens perform differently. There are fan ovens, fan assisted ovens, and none fan ovens. In my experience, they all take a little time to get up to temperature. Always preheat the oven; and generally the top of the oven is hotter than the bottom. All of the recipes in this book require a moderate heat of 170 degrees Celsius or gas mark 3. This saves fiddling around with the settings.

It's important to learn where the positions are on your particular oven so you can set the temperature accurately at 170 degrees or gas mark 3. On my oven, 170 degrees is at six o'clock.

Notes on hob temperatures

I have an analogue hob with knobs. I regard each knob as a clock:

- Between one o'clock and three o'clock is a low heat.

- Between three o'clock and six o'clock is a moderate heat.
- Between six o'clock and ten o'clock is a high heat.

Every hob is different, but by using the clock system you will get to know the best knob positions for cooking.

Notes on quantities

Generally, the quantities are described in teaspoons, dessertspoons, serving spoons or tablespoons, half-pint mugs and handfuls. Unless you have talking kitchen scales, there is no point trying to weigh anything. Establish which spoons and mug you are going to use and your measures will be consistent.

The tricky one is how to measure out oil. Less is usually better than more, and I talk about just a 'splash' of oil, which is about a dessertspoon; hardly technical, but as you do more cooking you will get better at judging how much to use!

I'm going to show you how to do basic cooking which will produce tasty food. If you want to progress on to more advanced cooking, then you will definitely need talking scales. (These will enable you to follow a more conventional cookbook too.)

In summary, the first part of the book will hopefully help you set up your kitchen so that, as a blind person, you can operate easily, freely and above all safely. This is not, when you think about it, a bad position to be in whether you can see or not.

It's all about reducing food preparation to a drill, or 'standing operating procedure'. Once the drill is mastered, then you'll be able to focus on the job in hand: making simple, good food that is nutritious.

If you think you can skip this first bit, think again! Tedious as it may be, and however adept you think you are, there is always more to learn. I have learned this the hard way!

CONFIDENCE AND CONCENTRATION

'When we can see, we do things blindly.'

– Kuffy Charles, 2019, daughter

The aim of this book is to enable you to feel confident in the kitchen, whether making yourself a drink or preparing food, and I will describe how to prepare the simplest of things, like a cup of tea, to creating all sorts of great meals. This will introduce you to the principles of kitchen safety and food preparation in action, and get you ready for super-organised drinks and meals with (hopefully) no dramas! Each recipe, and the principles required to prepare and cook it, will be a reminder of the degree to which you have to concentrate on what you are doing.

The meals will require more work from

you as they go on. But the intention is to lead you with simple steps so you can cook and enjoy basic food with confidence. If at the end you can say 'What was all the fuss about?' then we have a result!

LET'S BEGIN!

All journeys start with a single step, and the very first one on the transition to being able to cook is to make a cup of tea (which can easily be adapted to make a cup of coffee). It might seem like a really simple thing, but even this allows me to demonstrate the principles of **SLOPE** – safety, lazy person, organisation, preparation and execution – in practice.

Curiously, it would appear that not everyone can make tea. I heard there is a demonstration on making tea on YouTube, by Americans. Americans demonstrating to viewers how to make a British cup of tea! Really? Oh dear oh dear, oh dear.

Let me stress that putting a teabag in cold water and heating it only produces something quite unspeakable! So, let's make a good cup of tea, the British way!

P.S. Just for the record, our cousins across the Pond thought the best thing for a cup of tea was to tip it into Boston Harbor.

THE RECIPES

CATCH YOUR RABBIT #1

Making a cup of tea
(easy)

Making a good cup of tea

Objective: Learning to manage hot water and master organisation skills.

Hot tip: Always work within the tray to contain mess!

So, not forgetting *safety, lazy person principle and organisation*, this is how to proceed:

Organisation

Check you have the equipment – kettle, mug, spoon, bowl for used teabag – and a place to make the tea. (I am not a fan of lifting heavy kettles and trying to pour boiling water into a cup I cannot see. I use a one-cup kettle or an urn.)

Check you have the ingredients – teabag (or coffee), water, milk and sugar (if required).

Preparation

• Put bowl of hot soapy water in the sink

and a clean towel nearby.
- Wash and dry hands thoroughly.
- Check worktop is clean and clear.
- Ensure tray is in place on worktop.
- Put a large bowl nearby for rubbish.
- Place equipment on the worktop close to the tray.
- Place ingredients on the worktop close to the tray.
- Make sure the kettle has water in it.
- Place the cup or mug on the tray, and a spoon.
- Put the milk, tea or coffee near the tray, and sugar if you need it.

Execution

- Wash and dry your hands thoroughly.
- Put teabag in the mug and place by the kettle.
- Wait for water to boil and pour into mug.
- Place full mug on tray.
- Allow tea to steep.
- Remove teabag and place in the bowl.
- Put milk into mug. (I usually pour milk over finger to gauge the amount.)
- Put sugar in mug if required.

- Stir.

The tea is now ready to drink, but clear away any mess – put the milk back in the fridge, the teaspoon in the sink, and wipe the tray if you spilt anything – before you drink it.

It sounds like a lot of fuss. However, if you follow the principles of safety, lazy person principle, organisation, preparation and execution of making even a simple cup of tea you have the basis to make any meal.

Exactly the same principles and method can be applied here when making a cup of coffee. Just substitute a teabag for a teaspoon of your preferred brand.

Practice making a cup of tea (or coffee) several times a day! You'll be amazed how much easier it gets if you stay mindful and really concentrate on each stage of the process.

CATCH YOUR RABBIT #2

Beefing up ready meals
(easy to moderate)

RECIPE 1:

Chili con carne ready meal
with baked potato

Objective: Learning to manage a couple of things at once.

Hot tip: If you burn or scald yourself get the area into cold water as quickly as possible.

I will be using Parsley Box ready meals. I have used them before and like them as there is plenty of choice. They're good quality, with quick delivery, and quick to prepare. They're also reasonably priced, can be stored in a cupboard for up to six months, and are made in the UK with no artificial additives. But there are, of course, other brands available.

Before doing anything in the kitchen we must remember the vital principles: *safety, lazy person principle and organisation.* These are a constant requirement, and the day you forget or overlook them you might not be quite as successful, and may even end up injured.

Organisation

Gather equipment – sharp knife, butter knife, 2 teaspoons, clean tea towel, large bowl for rubbish.

Gather ingredients – [Parsley Box] ready meal, baked potato, butter or spread, and flavouring **(optional)**.

Hot tip: Have a mixing bowl handy to put any rubbish in. This prevents having to go to the waste bin when working.

Preparation

- Put bowl of hot soapy water in the sink and a clean towel nearby.
- Wash and dry hands thoroughly.
- Check worktop is clean and clear.
- Ensure tray is in place on worktop.
- Put a large bowl nearby for rubbish.
- Place equipment on the worktop close to the tray.
- Place ingredients on the worktop close to the tray.

Execution (remember to put all rubbish in the large bowl)

- Preheat oven to 170 degrees or gas mark 3.
- Remove cardboard sleeve on ready meal and pierce cover with a fork (to release steam when cooking).
- Wash and dry hands thoroughly.
- Pierce medium to large potato on all sides and put in microwave. Cook on high power for 5 minutes.
- When the microwave pings, remove the potato using a clean tea towel (oven gloves can get very grubby and are OK for dishes but not food) and turn over and put back into the microwave for 5 more minutes. When it pings, pass a knife through the potato. If it is soft all the way through it is done; if not, cook for another couple of minutes. (Obviously, the bigger the potato(es) the more time required.)
- Once the potato is soft, place in the preheated oven to crisp up for about 20 minutes.
- When the potato is in the oven place ready meal container in microwave

and cook as directed. When completed, leave to rest for a couple of minutes.

- Put serving bowl or plate to warm in oven for a couple of minutes. **Note**: I don't get these out of the cupboard until I need them right at the end to avoid clutter on the worktop.
- Remove baked potato from oven with clean tea towel and put into the bowl (or on the plate) and cut across in the top of the potato. Pull slightly apart with two teaspoons (as it will be very hot) and put a knob of butter inside.
- **Optional**: I add a good dollop of chopped chili to this as I like well spiced food. A little will give it an extra zing; a lot will make your eyes water!
- Using the clean tea towel remove the ready meal from the microwave and tip over the potato.

There you have it! A good, solid and nourishing meal.

RECIPE 2:

A baked potato with various fillings

Objective: Practising the basics of making yourself a baked potato, but with all sorts of fillings.

Hot tip: Use a clean tea towel rather than oven gloves when directly handling hot food like baked potatoes.

A baked potato is very versatile as it can be used as a main meal, part of a main meal, or as a snack.

Baked potatoes go well with:

- Grated cheese (chili flakes - optional)
- Baked beans (heat in saucepan for a couple of minutes)
- Tuna and sweetcorn mixed with mayonnaise (mix a tin of tuna with a handful of sweetcorn and add a dollop of mayonnaise and mix well)
- Cottage cheese and chives (add a

teaspoon of dried chives to cottage cheese and mix well)

To name only a few! There are no limits, really; just use your imagination.

Alternatively, the contents of the potato can be scooped out and mixed with any of the above and then returned to the potato skins.

As before, there is a wide range of ready meals that can be heated up and eaten with a baked potato. Basically, have fun with it and add whatever you like!

RECIPE 3:

Irish stew ready meal
with mashed potatoes
and peas (optional)

Objective: Learning to make mashed potatoes.

Hot tip: Always lay knives down
with the blade pointing
away from you.

As always, we must tend to the basics of **safety, lazy person and organisation** *before we start any food preparation. (Which I will now refer to as the* **SLO** *principle!)*

Organisation

Gather equipment – two mixing bowls, small saucepan, colander, fork, knife, plate, clean tea towel, large bowl for rubbish.

Gather ingredients – [Parsley Box] Irish stew, 2 or 3 potatoes depending on size, and butter or spread. **Optional**: salt and pepper, 1 egg, cheese, small onion, half a cup of peas.

Preparation

- Put bowl of hot soapy water in the sink and a clean towel nearby.
- Wash and dry hands thoroughly.
- Check worktop is clean and clear.
- Ensure tray is in place on worktop.
- Put a large bowl nearby for rubbish.
- Place equipment on the worktop close to the tray.
- Place ingredients on the worktop close to the tray.

Execution (remember to put all rubbish in the large bowl)

- Preheat oven to 170 degrees or gas mark 3.
- Wash and dry hands thoroughly.
- Pierce the potatoes and put in microwave for 5 minutes each potato on high power.
- Test the potatoes with sharp knife. If soft, put in oven to crisp up for about 20 minutes. If not, turn them over and give them a couple more minutes in

microwave.

- Remove sleeve of ready meal, pierce cover, put in microwave and cook as directed. When finished leave to rest.
- Put bowl or plate to warm in oven for a couple of minutes.
- Take potatoes from oven and place on work tray. Cut in half lengthways and scoop contents of each half into mixing bowl.
- Add butter or spread and mix with a fork until smooth and there are no lumps, and salt and pepper if desired.
- Put mashed potatoes onto the plate and pour ready meal on plate also.

At this stage you have basic mashed potatoes. If you want to be adventurous, add grated cheese, chopped onion, chili, nutmeg or beat an egg into the mashed potatoes. Don't be afraid to experiment! If you fancy some peas with this meal, cover the ready meal and mash with foil to keep warm and:

- Put some water in a small saucepan and bring to the boil. When boiling add peas.

- Turn down the heat and allow to cook for about 5 minutes.
- Drain into the colander over the sink and tip onto plate.

There you have it! Irish stew with mashed potatoes and peas. Add a cup of tea and a couple of rounds of bread and butter, if you fancy, and you have a very decent meal!

Hot tip: Peas are no friend for someone with sight loss. However, if you mix them into your mashed potatoes they are perfectly manageable!

RECIPE 4:

Chinese chicken
ready meal with rice

Objective: Learning to cook great rice (and egg fried rice if you fancy being more adventurous).

Hot tip: Dry rice swells to twice its size when cooked.

*Please keep the **SLO** principles at the front of your mind: **safety, lazy person principle and organisation.***

Organisation

Gather equipment – medium saucepan, sieve, clean tea towel, large bowl for rubbish. **If making egg fried rice** – large jug, chopping board, 3 small bowls, wok or frying pan, wooden spoon and spatula, fork, half-pint mug and vegetable knife, small mixing bowl.

Gather ingredients – [Parsley Box] Chinese chicken ready meal, rice. **Optional:** onion, mushroom, egg, peas, butter or oil, milk, salt and pepper.

Preparation

- Put bowl of hot soapy water in the sink and a clean towel nearby.
- Wash and dry hands thoroughly.
- Check worktop is clean and clear.
- Ensure tray is in place on worktop.
- Put a large bowl nearby for rubbish.
- Place equipment on the worktop close to the tray.
- Place ingredients on the worktop close to the tray.

Execution (remember to put all rubbish in the large bowl)

- Remove sleeve of ready meal, pierce cover with a fork, and place in microwave oven. Do not cook at this stage.
- Wash and dry hands thoroughly.
- Pour rice into mug until half full (use fingers as a guide).
- Pour rice into saucepan and add two mugs of water. Place on hob and bring to boil. Make sure you stir occasionally

to prevent rice sticking to pan. Allow to simmer for a couple of minutes, remove from hob and drain through a sieve with cold water to remove starch.

- Put back in the pan and add water and drain again.
- Put back in the pan and add two mugs of water. Return to hob and bring to boil.
- Turn down the heat and allow to simmer for 10 minutes.
- Allow to stand for a couple of minutes and taste. If still a little crunchy, cook for a little longer.
- If cooked to your liking, drain into a sieve.
- Put bowl or plate to warm in oven for a couple of minutes.
- Cook ready meal as directed. Plate up with rice.

EGG FRIED RICE

If you want egg fried rice, then drain rice and put to one side. Then:

- Chop half an onion into small pieces and

place in small bowl.

- Quarter some button mushrooms and put in a small bowl.
- Defrost some peas and place in a bowl.
- Beat one egg with a little milk in a small mixing bowl, and add salt and pepper to taste.
- Put wok or frying pan on the heat with a splash of oil (about a dessertspoon) or knob of butter. Wait for oil or butter to get hot – you'll be able to hear it sizzling – then tip bowl of chopped onions into pan. Turn with spatula to make sure onions are well coated.
- Keep turning for a couple of minutes and then tip in the mushrooms. Keep turning for a couple of minutes, and then remove from heat.
- Pour drained rice into pan and mix. Return to medium heat, turning slowly all the time for about 5 minutes.
- Remove from heat, push rice to one side of the pan and pour egg mixture into cleared area in the pan. It should cook just from the heat of the pan. When the egg mixture stops sizzling, turn it over. After a minute or so break up the mini omelette and mix into rice, onion and

mushrooms.

- Add peas and return whole mixture to a medium heat for a couple of minutes, turning all the time.
- Remove wok or frying pan from heat.
- Put bowl or plate to warm in oven for a couple of minutes.
- Cook ready meal in the microwave as directed.
- Put rice on plate and add ready meal when it is cooked.

**Hot tip: When turning|
food in a wok or frying pan
turn into the centre.**

RECIPE 5:

Chicken and bacon pie ready meal with pasta salad

Objective: Learning to cook pasta and make it into a delicious salad.

Hot tip 1: Pasta swells half as big again when cooked.

Hot tip 2: I always use dried pasta, which takes about 10 minutes to cook (but check the packet on this, as sometimes it's a little less or a little more). Fresh pasta takes just 2 to 3 minutes (maximum) to cook.

Please keep the **SLO** *principles at the front of your mind:* **safety, lazy person principle and organisation.**

Organisation

Gather equipment – large and small saucepan, large mixing bowl, colander or sieve, wooden spoon, slotted spoon, vegetable knife, plastic beaker or glass, clean tea towel, large bowl for rubbish.

Gather ingredients – [Parsley Box] chicken and bacon pie ready meal, penne pasta, oil, mayonnaise, spring onions, bell pepper, baby plum tomatoes, raisins, button mushrooms, garlic, white wine, sweetcorn, peas, chopped chili, butter, salt and pepper.

Preparation

- Put bowl of hot soapy water in the sink and a clean towel nearby.
- Wash and dry hands thoroughly.
- Check worktop is clean and clear.
- Ensure tray is in place on worktop.
- Put a large bowl nearby for rubbish.
- Place equipment on the worktop close to the tray.
- Place ingredients on the worktop close to the tray.

Execution (remember to put all rubbish in the large bowl)

- Remove sleeve from ready meal,

pierce covering with fork and place in microwave. Do not cook at this stage.

- Wash and dry hands thoroughly.
- Take a medium-sized handful of raisins (or sultanas) from the bag and put into mixing bowl of cold water and wash.
- Remove from cold water with slotted spoon and put into clean plastic beaker and cover with wine.
- Half fill small saucepan with water and put on hob to boil.
- Do the same for large saucepan. Put drop of oil into large pan to prevent pasta sticking.
- When water is boiling, drop a medium-sized handful of sweetcorn and peas into small pan and turn the heat down so that the water just simmers. Cook for no more than 5 minutes, then take off the heat. Drain through colander and leave to cool.
- When large pan of water is boiling, drop 2 large handfuls of pasta (penne, fusilli or medium shells; I prefer penne) into the water and turn down to simmer for 10 minutes or cooking time on packet. Stir occasionally.
- During that time, take 6 to 8 button

mushrooms and cut in half. Skin and slice three cloves of garlic.

- Cut some butter off the end of the block, about a quarter of an inch, and put in small saucepan. When melted, drop in the garlic and allow to simmer for 3 or 4 minutes. (Do not allow to burn as it will go bitter.) After 4 minutes or so, add the mushrooms. Swish saucepan around above the heat, as this makes sure mushrooms get well covered in the butter. Do this several times while you attend to the pasta.
- Take both saucepans off the heat. Taste pasta. It should be firm but not rubbery. If texture is OK, drain through a colander and fill saucepan with cold water and put pasta back in to stop it cooking. Put to one side, but not on hob.
- Take 4 spring onions and cut off base with roots and an inch off the leaves (this is called 'top and tailing') and remove first layer of skin. Wash in cold water in mixing bowl. Dice up the spring onions with vegetable knife and leave on chopping board.
- Empty the water out of the mixing bowl. Wash and dry with kitchen paper. Put

back on worktop.

- Tip peas and sweetcorn from colander into bowl. Empty pasta from large saucepan into colander. Drain well and put pasta into mixing bowl with peas and sweetcorn.
- Pour the butter, garlic and mushrooms on to the pasta.
- Mix contents of bowl together.
- Take 6 to 8 baby plum tomatoes, slice them lengthways and add to pasta mix.
- Take bell pepper, cut in half lengthways, remove seeds and slice into thin strips. Add to the pasta mix.
- Add half a teaspoon of chopped chili **(optional)** and serving spoon of mayonnaise.
- Add raisins. Drink wine, which tastes strange, but who cares. Add spring onions.
- Mix contents of bowl well. Add salt and pepper and mix well again. Use your hands if you wish, but wash them afterwards! **Note**: Using your hands and getting 'down and dirty' with the food is a great way of connecting with what you're doing. Rumour has it that it is we who bite the food, not the other

way around!

- Put bowl of pasta mix in the fridge to cool.
- Tidy up the work area, wash up any pots and leave to dry.
- Cook ready meal as directed.
- Leave to rest.
- Remove pasta mix from fridge and put some on plate. Add ready meal, and you have a really nutritious meal.

There should be enough pasta salad for another meal later, so cover dish with foil and put back in the fridge.

Hot tip: Always put lids back on jars – like mayonnaise – immediately after use so they don't get mixed up!

Section summary

I hope you've enjoyed trying some of these easy to moderate recipes. They have been designed to improve your concentration skills in the kitchen, whether sight-impaired or blind or just wanting to learn to cook, and get used to preparing basic carbohydrates to add to your ready meals. This is a great achievement and you should be proud of what you've already learnt!

*With the principles of **KISS – Keep It Simple Stupid** – and **SLOPE – Safety, Lazy person principle, Organisation, Preparation and Execution** – it is possible to cook without maiming yourself in the process!*

Now that you're familiar with heating up ready meals, preparing a baked potato or mashed potatoes, or cooking rice and pasta, do you feel ready to tackle some meals of your own?

I hope so!

NOTES

CATCH YOUR RABBIT #3

*Variations with Derbyshire oatcakes
(easy to moderate)*

RECIPE 6:

Oatcakes rolled with cheese

Objective: To introduce you to the humble oatcake and how to make a really tasty meal or snack with them.

Hot tip: Clear everything not in use from the worktop.

*Please keep the **SLO** principles at the front of your mind: **safety, lazy person principle and organisation.** If you find this a bit tedious, the A&E Department of the local hospital is even more so!*

The oatcake is a pancake-type of object made primarily of oats and found mainly in Staffordshire and Derbyshire. It is possible to make a reasonable substitute, which is more of an oat pancake. I have been trying to make them for nearly 40 years. Of course, being a man, I have not sought advice!

Organisation

Gather equipment – metal baking tray, teaspoon, chopping board, foil, clean tea towel, large bowl for rubbish.

Gather ingredients – 2 or 3 oatcakes, grated cheese, salt and pepper.

Preparation

- Put bowl of hot soapy water in the sink and a clean towel nearby.
- Wash and dry hands thoroughly.
- Check worktop is clean and clear.
- Ensure tray is in place on worktop.
- Put a large bowl nearby for rubbish.
- Place equipment on the worktop close to the tray.
- Place ingredients on the worktop close to the tray.

Execution (remember to put all rubbish in the large bowl)

- Pre-heat oven to 170 degrees or gas mark 3.
- Select baking tray and line with tin foil.

Place baking tray inside work tray.

- Wash and dry hands thoroughly.
- Place the first oatcake on the work tray at one end.
- Spread grated cheese over the oatcake. Add salt and pepper to taste.
- Take the edge of the oatcake nearest you and roll into a tube. Press moderately to prevent it unrolling.
- Take second oatcake and place in the gap in your work tray. Spread grated cheese over it and add salt and pepper to taste. Roll and press as before. Slide it over next to the first one.
- Put the final oatcake (if you're having 3) in the gap inside work tray. Spread grated cheese over it and salt and pepper, and roll and press as before.
- Transfer the oatcakes to the baking tray. You can smear them with butter if you wish!
- Put the baking tray in preheated oven for 12 to 15 minutes.
- Put bowl or plate to warm in oven for a couple of minutes.
- Remove and serve.

It is possible to make more exciting versions

of this. For example, after spreading the cheese on the oatcakes you could add:

- Chili – chopped chili from Sainsbury's is delicious. A little adds a zing; a lot makes your eyes water.
- Garlic and herbs – lazy garlic from Sainsbury's is great.
- Spring onion – top and tail and remove the outer layer, wash in cold water and chop into pieces (this is called dicing). Scatter on top of cheese.
- Previously cooked sausage split lengthways can be put on cheese so the oatcakes can still be rolled up.
- Slice chicken into thin strips, not forgetting to use your meat chopping board and a different knife, and put in a dish with lazy ginger from Sainsbury's.
- Heat a small splash of oil (about a dessertspoon) in a wok or frying pan, and once hot put in the chicken and ginger and stir-fry, which means to keep turning the mixture in the hot oil for 4 or 5 minutes, and then remove and spread on kitchen paper. Remove as much oil as possible and pour over the cheese.

What you have here is a 'Midlands fajita', as I call it, or a 'wrap', which is a really tasty snack. Basically, just use your imagination. I have even tried Marmite! Interesting, but rather strange!

If you want to turn oatcakes into a bigger meal, you could try the following:

- In the space between the oatcakes on the baking tray you can place chopped peppers, onion, cauliflower florets and small, boiled (in hot water on the hob for between 10 to 15 minutes) new potatoes brushed with garlic oil. You could also boil larger potatoes, if you prefer, for about 15 minutes, then quarter them, brush with oil and place on the tray to roast.
- Alternatively, you could put a couple of tomatoes, some beetroot, pickles, olives, peppers and salad leaves on the plate with the oatcakes.
- With the rolled oatcakes (and a buttered roll if you need something else to fill up on) and a cup of tea, this is a very satisfying meal.

Always use your imagination and choose what you like to eat.

RECIPE 7:

Breakfast oatcakes

Another delicious – and my favourite! – alternative is to pile scrambled eggs, mushrooms and bacon on one half of the pancake, fold it over, sprinkle cheese on the top and put in the oven for 15 minutes!

There are two ways of making scrambled eggs: in the microwave or in a saucepan. Following all of the previous advice on *safety, lazy person principle, organisation, preparation and execution,* this is how to make delicious breakfast oatcakes:

Using the microwave for scrambled eggs

- Preheat the oven to 170 degrees. Put some foil on a baking tray and place some bacon rashers on the foil. Put the tray in the oven and cook for 5 minutes.
- Meanwhile, break 2 eggs into a mixing bowl with a little milk and salt and pepper and mix together with a fork. Add a knob of butter.
- Put bowl in microwave on high power for 2 minutes.

- Remove and stir.
- Add chopped mushrooms and put back in microwave for 2 minutes.
- Remove and stir. If you like your scrambled eggs a bit sloppy, it might be cooked enough for you; if not, put back in the microwave for another minute.
- Remove, stir, and spread on half the oatcake.
- Turn the bacon over on the baking tray and put back in the oven for another 5 minutes.
- Remove and put on top of the scrambled eggs and mushrooms.
- Fold the oatcake over and sprinkle with cheese and put in oven for 5 to 6 minutes.
- Put bowl or plate to warm in oven for a couple of minutes and serve.

Using a saucepan for scrambled eggs:

- Preheat the oven to 170 degrees. Put some foil on a baking tray and place some bacon rashers on the foil. Put the tray in the oven and cook for 5 minutes.
- Put a knob of butter into the saucepan and melt.

- Break 2 eggs into a mixing bowl with a little milk and salt and pepper and mix together with a fork.
- Add the egg mixture and chopped mushrooms to the melted butter and cook over a gentle heat, stirring all the time.
- Turn the bacon over.
- When cooked to your taste, put the scrambled eggs and mushrooms on the oatcake, top with the bacon. Fold the oatcake over and sprinkle with grated cheese and put in oven for 5 to 6 minutes.
- Put bowl or plate to warm in oven for a couple of minutes.

Another way is to use the oatcake as a breakfast wrap:

- Put the oatcakes into the oven for 4 minutes to warm.
- Remove and place the cooked ingredients down the middle of the of the oatcake.
- Fold the edge nearest you to the middle, and then bring the farthest edge from you over the top and press down. Sprinkle with cheese and put in

the oven for 5 to 6 minutes.

This is such a tasty snack, so go wild and experiment!

RECIPE 8:

Derbyshire oatcake substitute

Again, following all of the previous advice on *safety, lazy person principle, organisation, preparation and execution,* this is how to make an oatcake substitute (which I'm still practising!):

Equipment – mixing bowl, wooden spoon, frying pan.

Ingredients – 1 heaped serving spoon of plain flour, 3 serving spoons of porridge oats, or any other oats, milk, 1 egg, salt and pepper.

Execution (remember to put all rubbish in the large bowl)

- Put the plain flour and oats in a bowl and mix. Add milk gradually and keep mixing.
- When the mixture is still quite thick, add an egg and salt and pepper.
- Mix thoroughly, and add milk until mixture has the consistency of runny

custard.

- Heat a splash of oil (a dessertspoon) in a frying pan.
- Pour some of the mixture into the frying pan and move the frying pan about so the mixture covers the whole of the bottom of the pan with a thin layer.
- Put back on the heat for about 1 minute. Keep frying pan moving to prevent sticking.
- Turn it over and give it 10 to 20 seconds on the heat, then remove and slide onto a plate.
- Allow to cool and you have a reasonable substitute for a Derbyshire oatcake.

Be warned, the first one is generally not very good, so maybe make a little extra mixture to practice with!

It is also possible to make sweet versions. Substitute the salt and pepper for raisins or walnuts or chopped fruit – this is courtesy of my mate Doug!

Note: There are lots of recipes for oatcake substitutes online, so find one that suits you and enjoy!

NOTES

CATCH YOUR RABBIT #4

Great sausage meals
(easy to moderate)

RECIPE 9:

Sausage sandwich
with egg (optional)

Objective: Practising frying.

Hot tip 1: Use good
quality sausages.

Hot tip 2: Listen for sizzling to
let you know when the oil is
ready, and your sense of smell
for when the sausages are ready!
(This applies to cooking anything
and everything.)

Note: I use a wok or frying pan or the
oven to cook sausages as the grill can be
too fierce and burn them.

*Please keep the **SLO** principles at the front
of your mind: **safety, lazy person principle
and organisation.***

Organisation

Gather equipment – wok or frying pan,

spatula, tongs, sharp knife, chopping boards (one for vegetables and one for meat), clean tea towel, plate, kitchen paper, clean tea towel, large bowl for rubbish.

Gather ingredients – good sausages, bread or a bread roll, butter or spread, oil, onions, brown or red (tomato) sauce, or mustard to taste.

Preparation

- Put bowl of hot soapy water in the sink and a clean towel nearby.
- Wash and dry hands thoroughly.
- Check worktop is clean and clear.
- Ensure tray is in place on worktop.
- Put a large bowl nearby for rubbish.
- Place equipment on the worktop close to the tray.
- Place ingredients on the worktop close to the tray.

Execution (remember to put all rubbish in the large bowl)

- Put a splash of oil (about a dessertspoon) in the frying pan.

- Top, tail and skin onion and cut in half. Put one half in the fridge wrapped in foil. Slice the other half.
- Heat the oil and put onions into pan. Turn constantly for about 5 minutes.
- Remove pan from heat. Remove onion and place on kitchen paper on plate.
- Replace pan on heat.
- Prick sausages and place in pan. Keep turning for about 10 minutes.
- Remove pan from heat.
- Use tongs or a fork and put sausages on meat chopping board.
- Hold still with tongs or fork and cut sausages in half lengthways.
- Butter the bread (and put a smear of mustard on the bread if this is to your taste), place sausage halves on bread, add fried onions and a light dusting of salt and pepper.
- Add brown sauce or red (tomato) sauce to taste.
- Put second piece of bread on top, cut in half across the sausages.

You may wish to add a fried egg to the sandwich:

- Reheat the oil in the pan and break an egg into it.
- Fry for 2 to 3 minutes.
- If you like your eggs 'easy-over' turn egg over with spatula and cook for 1 minute.
- Remove and place on top of the other ingredients. Top with the second slice of bread.

Hot tip: Buy spreadable butter or take butter out of the fridge before using, and spread by scraping the knife right across the bread. Turn bread 90 degrees and repeat. Do this for all four sides. This way you can be sure of good coverage!

RECIPE 10:

Bangers and mash

Objective: Creating a classic sausage meal and making gravy.

Hot tip: Read or listen to all recipe instructions at least twice.

*Remember to keep it **SLO: safe, lazy, organised.***

Organisation

Gather equipment – medium saucepan, sharp knife, baking tray, spoon, clean tea towel, large bowl for rubbish.

Gather ingredients – good sausages, 2 or 3 medium potatoes, butter, salt and pepper, carrots, peas, gravy granules.

Preparation

- Put bowl of hot soapy water in the sink and a clean towel nearby.
- Wash and dry hands thoroughly.

- Check worktop is clean and clear.
- Ensure tray is in place on worktop.
- Put a large bowl nearby for rubbish.
- Place equipment on the worktop close to the tray.
- Place ingredients on the worktop close to the tray.

Execution (remember to put all rubbish in the large bowl)

- Preheat oven to 170 degrees or gas mark 3.
- Wash and dry hands thoroughly.
- Pierce potatoes and put in microwave on high power for 5 minutes each.
- Put sausages on baking tray (they'll need to cook for 30 minutes).
- Check potatoes and turn over and cook for another 5 minutes each, or until soft inside, and then put in the oven to crisp up with the sausages.
- Top and tail the carrots. Wash well and cut into slices lengthways. **Note:** I don't skin carrots or parsnips; washing is good enough.
- Put water into saucepan and add carrots. Bring to boil and then turn the

heat down to simmer for 5 minutes.

- Add the peas and bring back to boil.
- Turn down and simmer for 5 minutes and then remove from heat. Drain into colander, catching the hot water in another saucepan.
- Remove potatoes from oven, cut in half lengthways, scoop contents into mixing bowl and mash with a little butter, salt and pepper if to your taste.
- Put bowl or plate to warm in oven for a couple of minutes.
- Remove sausages from oven.
- Place sausages on plate, add mashed potatoes, peas and carrots.
- Use water from cooking vegetables to make gravy by adding gravy granules and stirring steadily whilst on the heat. Once the liquid becomes slightly resistant, the gravy is ready. Pour on to plate.

Hot tip: Use the water from cooking the vegetables to make gravy as it's tastier and contains nutrients from the vegetables.

RECIPE 11:

Wind in the Willows
(or 'Toad in the hole')

(Called Wind in the Willows because we have Toad (the sausage) and his three companions (the veg) with gravy the colour of the Thames near Toad Hall!)

Objective: Learning to make batter.

Hot tip: Do not touch electric plugs with wet hands!

*As always, apply the **SLO** principles to all that you do: **be safe, lazy and organised.***

Organisation

Gather equipment – mixing bowl, mug, sharp knife, tablespoon, small and medium saucepan, colander, kitchen paper, clean tea towel, large bowl for rubbish.

Gather ingredients – good sausages, plain flour, egg, milk, peas, carrots, medium to large potato, butter, gravy granules, oil,

94

salt and pepper.

Preparation

- Put bowl of hot soapy water in the sink and a clean towel nearby.
- Wash and dry hands thoroughly.
- Check worktop is clean and clear.
- Ensure tray is in place on worktop.
- Put a large bowl nearby for rubbish.
- Place equipment on the worktop close to the tray.
- Place ingredients on the worktop close to the tray.

Execution (remember to put all rubbish in the large bowl)

- Preheat oven to 170 degrees gas mark 3.
- Wash and dry hands thoroughly.
- Pierce potato and put in the microwave for 5 minutes on high power.
- Turn potato over and cook for another 5 minutes or until soft inside.
- Smear oil around inside of a high-sided ovenproof dish. Place 2 or 3 sausages in one end and put in oven for 10 minutes.

- Put potato in the oven to crisp up at the same time.

To make the batter

- To make the batter mix, put half a mug of plain flour in mixing bowl and a little salt. Gradually add a mug of milk, stirring continuously.
- Once mixture feels smooth, add an egg. Continue to mix until smooth.
- Take dish from oven.
- Pour batter mixture into dish and replace in oven.
- Cook for a further 25 minutes.

And on with the rest

- Put some water in the small saucepan.
- Top, tail and wash carrots, and cut into strips lengthways (called batons). Add to the saucepan.
- Bring to boil and then turn down heat and simmer for 5 minutes. Remove from heat, add peas and bring back to boil and cook for a further 5 minutes.
- Drain and save the water in a small saucepan.

- Remove dish with sausages and batter from oven. The batter should have risen to fill dish.
- Put the drained carrots and peas in the other half of the dish.
- Make gravy as previously described by adding gravy granules to the saved vegetable water and heating, stirring all the time.
- Take the potato out of the oven using a clean tea towel. Put in the dish with the sausages, batter and veg. Cut open and put a knob of butter on top. Pour on the gravy. You can eat this straight out of the dish, but be careful as it will be very hot! Alternatively, put bowl or plate to warm in oven for a couple of minutes and transfer food to warm plate.

This fantastic meal can also be made for more than one person by filling the bottom of the dish with sausages, and serving the vegetables and potatoes separately rather than putting them in with the sausages and batter.

Hot tip: When cooking batter
– or Yorkshire pudding, as it's
called – the dish must be very
hot before pouring in the batter.
It goes without saying that
great care must be taken when
handling a dish this hot.

RECIPE 12:

A semi-healthy
sausage breakfast!

Objective: Learning to cook several things at once.

Hot tip: Be methodical and remain focussed at all times.

As always, stay **SLO: safe, lazy and organised.**

Organisation

Gather equipment – medium saucepan, oven tray with rack, wok or frying pan, 2 medium mixing bowls, tin opener, sharp knife, fork, clean tea towel, large bowl for rubbish.

Gather ingredients – sausages, bacon, eggs, tomatoes, mushrooms, butter, potatoes, tin of baked beans, bread, salt and pepper.

Preparation

- Put bowl of hot soapy water in the sink and a clean towel nearby.
- Wash and dry hands thoroughly.
- Check worktop is clean and clear.
- Ensure tray is in place on worktop.
- Put a large bowl nearby for rubbish.
- Place equipment on the worktop close to the tray.
- Place ingredients on the worktop close to the tray.

Execution (remember to put all rubbish in the large bowl)

- Preheat oven to 170 degrees or gas mark 3.
- Wash and dry hands thoroughly.
- Pierce sausages, place on rack in baking tray and put in oven for 15 minutes.
- Cut tomatoes in half.
- Turn sausages, and add bacon and halved tomatoes to rack, and return to oven for 10 minutes.
- After 10 minutes turn bacon and return tray to oven for 10 more minutes.
- Pierce potatoes and place in microwave

on high power for 5 minutes, turn over, then 5 minutes more or until cooked.

- Mix eggs with a splash of milk in mixing bowl.
- Chop some mushrooms and add to eggs, and add salt and pepper and a knob of butter.
- When potatoes are done place in oven to crisp up for about 20 minutes.
- Put mixing bowl with eggs into microwave on high power for 2 minutes.
- Remove, mix again, and replace in microwave for 2 more minutes.
- Remove and mix, and put back in microwave to rest.
- Remove potatoes from oven, halve and scoop contents into mixing bowl and mix with butter, salt and pepper.
- Put bowl or plate to warm in oven for a couple of minutes.
- Alternatively, mix with eggs and fry in wok or frying pan. If not, remove plate from oven and put the mashed potatoes on it.
- Tip contents of small can of beans into saucepan, and heat through. Stir to prevent burning. Once the beans bubble, remove from heat.

- Take tray out of oven and put sausages, bacon and tomatoes on plate with potato.
- Microwave eggs for another half minute, remove, mix and place on plate.
- Pour beans onto the plate. Add buttered bread if you like.

And there you have it, sausage, bacon, tomatoes, mashed potatoes, scrambled eggs, baked beans and bread and butter!

Note on quantities: For one person I suggest 2 sausages and 2 rashers of bacon, 1 tomato, and 1 small to medium potato, plus a small tin of baked beans.

**Hot tip: Always warm the plate.
A hot plate is vital for keeping
food warm while you fiddle about
with last-minute items like bread
and butter.**

NOTES

CATCH YOUR RABBIT #5

Delicious pasta meals
(easy to moderate)

RECIPE 13:

Macaroni cheese

Objective: Learning to make great cheese sauce.

Hot tip 1: Hot cheese can blister your mouth. Be careful! (I know this from experience!)

Hot tip 2: All pasta dishes can be made with gluten-free pasta if required.

Hot tip 3: English mustard brings out the flavour of the cheese, but not too much, you only need a little.

As always, apply rules of SLO: stay safe, lazy and organised.

Organisation

Gather equipment – medium saucepan, large saucepan, colander, wooden spoon, 2 small bowls, ovenproof dish, sharp knife, tablespoon, half-pint mug, clean tea towel, large bowl for rubbish.

Gather ingredients – mug and a half of macaroni, grated cheese, medium onion, butter, milk, mushrooms, tomatoes, plain flour, salt and pepper, mustard and red (tomato) sauce **(optional).**

Preparation

- Put bowl of hot soapy water in the sink and a clean towel nearby.
- Wash and dry hands thoroughly.
- Check worktop is clean and clear.
- Ensure tray is in place on worktop.
- Put a large bowl nearby for rubbish.
- Place equipment on the worktop close to the tray.
- Place ingredients on the worktop close to the tray.

Execution (remember to put all rubbish in the large bowl)

- Wash and dry hands thoroughly.
- Half fill large saucepan and put on to hob to boil. Put a drop of oil in water

(this stops the pasta from sticking together).

- When water is boiling tip macaroni into pan, turn down heat and simmer for 5 or 6 minutes, stirring occasionally.
- In the meantime, top and tail and skin and chop medium onion into small pieces. Put into small bowl.
- Halve mushrooms and put in second bowl.
- After 5 or 6 minutes remove macaroni and drain into colander. Rinse with cold water to stop the macaroni cooking and drain. Put to one side.
- Fill half-pint mug with milk.

To make the onion and cheese sauce

- Preheat oven to 170 degrees or gas mark 3.
- Put medium saucepan on the heat. Remove quarter of an inch of butter from block and drop into saucepan. Stir with wooden spoon until butter melts.
- When butter begins to bubble, put about a third of the onions into the butter. Stir to make sure all the onion is coated with butter. Remove pan from

heat after a minute or so.

- Drop in level tablespoon of plain flour and stir into the butter and onions. (This prevents the sauce from going lumpy.)
- Return to heat and keep stirring. Once it begins to thicken up, remove from heat.
- Pour in a little of the milk, stir thoroughly and return to heat. Keep stirring. When it thickens up again, pour in some more milk. Keep stirring. As it thickens up again, pour in rest of milk.
- Reduce heat and add the rest of the onions and the mushrooms. Keep stirring for another 5 minutes, then add a good handful of grated cheese.
- Keep stirring, then add some mixed herbs and a little English mustard.
- Stir for a couple of minutes, then remove from heat and leave to stand.
- If it seems very thick, stir in a little more milk, but not too much! The consistency should be like custard.

Back to the macaroni

- Put macaroni back into large saucepan.

Add onion and cheese sauce. Mix well with wooden spoon.

- **Optional**: Put a thin layer of red (tomato) sauce (or tomato puree) on the bottom of the ovenproof dish (inside, obviously).
- Pour everything into the ovenproof dish, smooth and cover with thinly sliced tomato. Dust with dried basil. Cover generously with grated cheese. Place in preheated oven for 15 minutes or until the cheese is melted and golden.
- Put bowl or plate to warm in oven for a couple of minutes.

You should have enough macaroni cheese for two or three people, and it'll go further still if you serve with a side salad.

Note: You can sprinkle the cheese with mixed herbs, or even paprika, at the end, which is a tasty, optional addition.

Hot tip: When making cheese sauce, keep stirring!

RECIPE 14:

Ham and cheese pasta meal

Objective: Practising doing a couple of things simultaneously.

Hot tip: The quantities for this dish are hard to judge for one person. You can either put the surplus in a labelled and dated airtight container in the freezer for another day, or invite someone over to share the meal with you.

As always, stay **SLO: safe, lazy and organised.**

Organisation

Gather equipment – large and medium saucepan, colander, ovenproof dish, sharp knife, wooden spoon, tablespoon, half-pint mug, clean tea towel, large bowl for rubbish.

Gather ingredients – cheese, ham, plain

flour, milk, butter, small onion, penne pasta, peas, mustard, garlic, mixed herbs, salt and pepper.

Preparation

- Put bowl of hot soapy water in the sink and a clean towel nearby.
- Wash and dry hands thoroughly.
- Check worktop is clean and clear.
- Ensure tray is in place on worktop.
- Put a large bowl nearby for rubbish.
- Place equipment on the worktop close to the tray.
- Place ingredients on the worktop close to the tray.

Execution (remember to put all rubbish in the large bowl)

- Preheat oven to 170 degrees or gas mark 3.
- Wash and dry hands thoroughly.
- Half fill large saucepan with water, add drop of oil and put on hob to bring to boil.
- Put about half an inch off the end of the block of butter into medium saucepan

to melt.

- Top and tail and skin and chop small onion into small pieces and put in pan with butter. Stir to coat onions, and keep on low heat for a couple of minutes.
- Put a mug and a half of penne pasta into boiling water in large saucepan. Simmer for 10 minutes, or the time stated on the packet, stirring occasionally.
- Remove pan with melted butter from heat and drop in level tablespoon of plain flour and stir into the butter and onions. (This prevents the sauce from going lumpy.)
- Return to heat and keep stirring. Once it begins to thicken up, remove from heat.
- Pour in a little of the milk, stir thoroughly and return to heat. Keep stirring. When it thickens up again, pour in some more milk. Keep stirring.
- As it thickens up again, pour in rest of milk, the mustard, the herbs and salt and pepper.
- Add the peas and stir.
- Remove pasta from heat when it's cooked and drain, then rinse with cold water and put to one side.

- Add small pieces of ham to the sauce.
- Add a good handful of grated cheese and stir for a couple of minutes.
- Remove from heat.
- Put pasta in large saucepan and pour sauce over. Mix well.
- **Optional**: Spread a little red (tomato) sauce (or tomato puree) on the bottom of the ovenproof dish (inside, obviously), and pour in pasta mixture. Smooth off and put in oven for no more than 15 minutes.
- Remove when ready and serve.

RECIPE 15:

Chicken pasta bake
(without sauce)

Objective: Learning to keep chopping boards for meat and vegetables separate.

Hot tip: The lids from tins or cans can be very sharp, so handle with care!

*As always, apply the **SLO** method of cooking: **stay safe, lazy and organised.***

Organisation

Gather equipment – wok or frying pan, large and medium saucepans, 5 dishes or bowls, 2 sharp knives, 2 chopping boards (one for meat and one for vegetables), wooden spoon, colander, medium-sized deep-sided ovenproof dish with lid, tin opener, clean tea towel, large bowl for rubbish.

Gather ingredients – diced chicken, tin of chopped tomatoes, cheese, courgette, broccoli, bell pepper, button mushrooms, medium onion, peas, sweetcorn, celery, penne pasta, oil or butter, lazy garlic, chili, basil, salt and pepper.

Use your imagination with ingredients. For instance, you might not be a fan of sweetcorn or mushrooms, so leave them out or replace them with something you like better. The above is only a basic suggestion.

Preparation

- Put bowl of hot soapy water in the sink and a clean towel nearby.
- Wash and dry hands thoroughly.
- Check worktop is clean and clear.
- Ensure tray is in place on worktop.
- Put a large bowl nearby for rubbish.
- Place equipment on the worktop close to the tray.
- Place ingredients on the worktop close to the tray.

Execution (remember to put all rubbish in the large bowl)

- Preheat oven to 170 degrees or gas

mark 3.
- Wash and dry hands thoroughly.
- Put meat chopping board into work tray. Take diced chicken pieces and halve each piece, then put in a bowl and mix with lazy garlic.
- Wash chopping board and knife thoroughly, and wash and dry hands.
- Wash or wipe the work tray.
- Put vegetable chopping board and vegetable knife into work tray.
- Wash courgette, top and tail, cut in half and split each half into eight batons and place in a bowl.
- Halve button mushrooms and place in bowl.
- Top and tail and skin and cut onion into small pieces and place in a bowl.
- Halve bell pepper lengthways, remove seeds, cut into thin strips and put in bowl.
- Take half a stick of celery, wash, cut leaves off the top and ragged bit off the bottom. Split into thin batons and put in a bowl.
- Carefully open tin of chopped tomatoes.
- Heat oil or butter in wok or frying pan and add chicken. Keep on high heat and

turn constantly.

- Add onion and keep turning.
- Add chopped tomato, put heat on medium, and keep turning. (Remember to dispose of the empty can and lid.)
- Add mushrooms and basil, peas and sweetcorn, and keep turning.
- Take off heat and add celery, pepper slices, courgette and a quarter of a teaspoonful of chopped chili. Mix well and leave to rest.
- Fill saucepan half full of water, add drop of oil and bring to boil. When boiling drop in mug and a half of penne, stir, then turn down heat and simmer for 5 minutes.
- Remove from heat, drain, return to saucepan.
- Add tomato puree, mix well.
- Add handful of grated cheese and mix well.
- Pour contents of wok or frying pan into pasta and mix well.
- Pour contents of saucepan into ovenproof dish, level, cover with grated cheese and put in oven for 40 minutes.
- Put bowl or plate to warm in oven for a couple of minutes.

Remove, serve and enjoy!

Hot tip: Make sure oven is up to heat before putting anything in.

RECIPE 16:

An indulgent pasta salad

Objective: It seems like there's a lot to do here, but in truth there isn't. It's just a question of learning to identify all the separate ingredients and how to chop them.

> **Hot tip**: When it comes to ingredients, you could try making a map in your head of where they all are on your worktop. One method is to use the clock system, and memorise mushrooms being at one o'clock, onions at two o'clock, and prawns at three o'clock, and so on.

*As always, apply **SLO** to your activities in the kitchen and **stay safe, lazy and organised**.*

Organisation

Gather equipment – wok or frying pan, large and small saucepan, 2 mixing bowls, sharp knife, spatula, wooden spoon, clean tea towel, large bowl for rubbish.

Gather ingredients – uncooked king prawns, smoked salmon, asparagus, button mushrooms, garlic, butter, oil, chili, peas, sweetcorn, baby plum tomatoes, bell pepper, spring onion, mayonnaise, mango pieces, red wine-soaked sultanas, walnut pieces, salt and pepper.

Preparation

- Put bowl of hot soapy water in the sink and a clean towel nearby.
- Wash and dry hands thoroughly.
- Check worktop is clean and clear.
- Ensure tray is in place on worktop.
- Put a large bowl nearby for rubbish.
- Place equipment on the worktop close to the tray.
- Place ingredients on the worktop close to the tray.

Execution (remember to put all rubbish in the large bowl)

- Wash and dry hands thoroughly

- Wash a handful of sultanas in cold water, put in plastic beaker or glass and cover with red wine.
- Half fill large saucepan with water, add a drop of oil and put on heat to boil.
- Put knob of butter in medium saucepan, then put on low heat to melt. Do not allow to burn.
- Take asparagus stalks, remove the top two inches and put to one side. Put the remaining stalks back into fridge.
- When the water in the large pan is boiling put a mug and a half of penne into the water, stir and reduce heat. Allow to simmer for 10 minutes or however long it recommends on the packet.
- When the pasta is cooked, drain into colander and allow to cool.
- Whilst the pasta is cooking, put asparagus tips into butter and gently simmer for 5 minutes. Remove and put into a small dish and set aside.
- Cut button mushrooms in half, and skin and slice garlic cloves. Drop garlic into butter and allow to simmer for a few minutes, then add mushroom halves. Move saucepan around to makes sure mushrooms are well coated with the

butter. Do this over the heat for 2 to 3 minutes, then remove saucepan from heat.

- Run cold water over the pasta, drain well and put in mixing bowl.
- Put mushrooms back on the heat to warm through and then tip over the pasta. Mix pasta and mushrooms well.
- Take the asparagus tips, wrap with smoked salmon and put in the bowl with the pasta.
- Wash medium saucepan. Half fill with water and put on the hob to boil.
- When boiling drop in a handful of peas and sweetcorn. Turn down and allow to simmer for 3 to 4 minutes.
- Remove from heat, drain, run cold water over them and allow to drain again.
- Put wok or frying pan on the heat with splash of oil.
- Once hot, add half a teaspoon of chopped ginger and allow to simmer in oil for 3 to 4 minutes.
- Increase heat and add the uncooked prawns. Keep them turning and moving in the pan for 2 to 3 minutes. Tip prawns onto a plate to cool.
- Top and tail the spring onions, remove

outer skin, dice and add to pasta.

- Take baby plum tomatoes, split into quarters lengthways, and add to pasta.
- Take bell pepper, cut in half lengthways, remove seeds and stalk, slice into thin strips and add to pasta.
- Add mango slices to pasta.
- Mix pasta and other ingredients thoroughly.
- Remove sultanas from wine, add to pasta, and drink wine!
- Add peas and sweetcorn to pasta and mix in.
- Add prawns.
- Add half a teaspoon of chopped chili **(optional)** and mix really well, then add heaped tablespoon of mayonnaise and mix well. You can use more if you wish.
- Put the bowl of pasta salad into the fridge for an hour.
- Remove and serve with chilled New Zealand white wine, which is particularly nice, or Oyster Bay white wine.

NOTES

CATCH YOUR RABBIT #6

Great rice meals
(moderate)

RECIPE 17:

Chicken, rice and peas

Objective: Learning to cook great rice.

Hot tip: Chicken is funny stuff, so to avoid cross contamination always use a separate chopping board.

Always apply the **SLO** *principles in the kitchen:* **stay safe, lazy and organised.**

Organisation

Gather equipment – wok or frying pan, small and large saucepans, half-pint mug, 2 sharp knives, 2 chopping boards (meat and veg), wooden spoon and spatula, colander, small dish, clean tea towel, large bowl for rubbish.

Gather ingredients – chicken fillet, rice, button mushrooms, peas, garlic, crème fraiche, oil or butter, salt and pepper.

Preparation

- Put bowl of hot soapy water in the sink and a clean towel nearby.
- Wash and dry hands thoroughly.
- Check worktop is clean and clear.
- Ensure tray is in place on worktop.
- Put a large bowl nearby for rubbish.
- Place equipment on the worktop close to the tray.
- Place ingredients on the worktop close to the tray.

Execution (remember to put all rubbish in the large bowl)

- Put half a mug of rice into large saucepan. Add two mugs of water and put on heat to boil.
- Once boiling turn down heat and allow to simmer for 5 minutes.
- Remove from heat, drain rice and wash through with cold water. Return to saucepan and put fresh water in and return to heat. Bring to boil and reduce heat and simmer for 10 minutes.
- Remove from heat and drain. Rest colander of rice on large saucepan and

put to one side.

- Dice chicken into fairly small pieces on the meat chopping board, place in small dish and put to one side.
- Wash meat chopping board and knife thoroughly. Wash and dry hands thoroughly.
- Put vegetable chopping board in the work tray.
- Put splash of oil into wok or frying pan and heat gently.
- Top and tail and skin three garlic cloves, split lengthways, and add to oil in wok or frying pan. Simmer for a couple of minutes, add chicken and increase heat, turning continuously for 5 minutes. Remove from heat.
- Halve button mushrooms. Add to wok or frying pan and return to heat. Keep turning for a couple of minutes.
- Add salt and pepper to taste.
- Add rice and mix well and reduce to moderate heat.
- Add half a mug of peas and mix well.
- Add crème fraiche and mix in well.
- Keep on a low heat for 5 minutes, turning occasionally.
- Put bowl or plate to warm in oven for a

couple of minutes.
- Turn off heat and allow to rest for a few minutes and then serve.

You can store the surplus in a labelled and dated airtight container and put in freezer when cold.

RECIPE 18:

A Spanish paella-type rice dish

Objective: A different way to cook rice.

Hot tip: Have someone check the contents of your fridge weekly to make sure there is nothing growing whiskers and about to growl at you!

As always, the SLO rules apply: safety, lazy person principle and organisation.

Organisation

Gather equipment – wok or frying pan, wooden spatula, 2 chopping boards (for meat and veg), 2 sharp knives, tin opener, 5 small dishes, clean tea towel, large bowl for rubbish.

Gather ingredients – diced chicken, medium onion, rice, oil, peas, mushrooms, bell pepper, tin of chopped tomatoes, sweetcorn, lazy garlic, lazy ginger, chili, mixed herbs, salt and pepper.

Preparation

- Put bowl of hot soapy water in the sink and a clean towel nearby.
- Wash and dry hands thoroughly.
- Check worktop is clean and clear.
- Ensure tray is in place on worktop.
- Put a large bowl nearby for rubbish.
- Place equipment on the worktop close to the tray.
- Place ingredients on the worktop close to the tray.

Execution (remember to put all rubbish in the large bowl)

- Wash and dry hands thoroughly.
- Put a good splash of oil in the wok or frying pan and put on moderate heat. Once warm add half a mugful of rice. Stir rice into oil for a few minutes and then remove from heat.
- Open tin of chopped tomatoes and add to wok or frying pan, return to heat and stir for a minute or so and remove from heat.
- Put the vegetable chopping board in the work tray and top and tail and skin

and chop onion and put in small dish or bowl.

- Slice and deseed a bell pepper and put in small bowl or dish.
- Put half a mug of peas into small dish.
- Put sweetcorn into small dish.
- Take out vegetable chopping board and put meat chopping board in work tray.
- Dice chicken and put in small bowl or dish.
- Add onions to wok or frying pan and return to heat. Stir and add mug of water.
- Add chicken, increase heat and keep turning for 5 minutes and then reduce heat to moderate.
- Add pepper slices and sweetcorn.
- Add mushrooms and peas, and keep turning for another 5 minutes.
- Allow to simmer for 5 minutes, then add half a teaspoon of chili, a teaspoon of lazy garlic, mixed herbs, salt and pepper and teaspoon of chopped ginger.
- Mix in well and allow to simmer for another 5 minutes.
- Turn off heat and allow to rest for 15 minutes.
- After 15 minutes put on high heat for a

couple of minutes, turning continuously.
- Put bowl or plate to warm in oven for a couple of minutes
- Remove from heat and serve.

Freeze any surplus in a labelled and dated airtight container.

Hot tip: You can always add more heat; it is impossible to take it away once applied. Therefore, always increase heat in small doses!

RECIPE 19:

A simple chicken curry

Objective: Learning to cook a great curry from scratch!

Hot tip: Make sure that everything you use is absolutely clean.

Always remember the **SLO** *principles:* **safety, lazy person principle and organisation.**

Organisation

Gather equipment – wok or frying pan, 5 small dishes, 1 medium to large dish, 2 chopping boards (one for meat and one for vegetables), large saucepan, colander, tin opener, 2 sharp knives, wooden spoon and spatula, half-pint mug, teaspoon, medium mixing bowl, clean tea towel, large bowl for rubbish.

Gather ingredients – diced chicken, rice, curry paste, ginger, chili, onions, chopped tomatoes, bell pepper, dried coconut, mango pieces, mushrooms, plain Greek yoghurt, raisins, cucumber, mint jelly, spring onions, salt and pepper.

Preparation

- Put bowl of hot soapy water in the sink and a clean towel nearby.
- Wash and dry hands thoroughly.
- Check worktop is clean and clear.
- Ensure tray is in place on worktop.
- Put a large bowl nearby for rubbish.
- Place equipment on the worktop close to the tray.
- Place ingredients on the worktop close to the tray.

Execution (remember to put all rubbish in the large bowl)

- Wash and dry hands thoroughly.
- Dice chicken into strips about size of half a little finger and put in medium to large dish. Add a dessert spoonful of curry paste, teaspoonful of chopped ginger, half a teaspoonful of chopped chili. Mix in well and put to one side.

- Wash and dry meat chopping board and knife thoroughly. Wash and dry hands thoroughly.
- Put half a mug of rice into large saucepan with two mugs of cold water and put onto boil, once boiling turn down heat and allow to simmer for 5 minutes.
- Remove from heat, drain and wash with cold water, refill water and put onto boil and simmer for 15 minutes.
- Remove from heat, drain and put aside.

To make the cucumber and yoghurt

- Whilst the rice is cooking, put vegetable chopping board and knife into the work tray.
- Cut a two-inch chunk of the cucumber and put remainder back in the fridge. Remove skin and dice cucumber into quarter-inch chunks and place in one of the small dishes.
- Add a spoonful of mint jelly and half the yoghurt and mix well. Put in the fridge.

And back to the curry

- Top and tail and skin and slice onion

and put into small dish.
- Halve and deseed bell pepper, slice into medium slices and put into small dish.
- Halve or quarter mushrooms depending on size and put in small dish.
- Open tin of chopped tomatoes, put to one side.
- Put wok or frying pan on heat, add splash of oil, allow to heat, and once hot put in chopped onions. Turn for a couple of minutes and remove from moderate heat.
- Add two teaspoons of curry paste, mix in well and return to the heat. Keep turning.
- After a couple of minutes, add chopped tomatoes. Allow to simmer, turning occasionally.
- Add chicken and raise heat. Turn continually for 10 minutes.
- Add raisins and bell peppers. Mix and turn occasionally.
- Add mushrooms and dried coconut. Mix and turn occasionally.
- Add the rest of the yoghurt and mix. Turn heat down to low and turn occasionally.
- Add mango pieces and mix in well.

- Top, tail and skin spring onions, split lengthways and mix into curry. Remove from heat.
- Put bowl or plate to warm in oven for a couple of minutes.
- Put water onto boil in large saucepan. When boiling, drop rice into it to heat through. Drain rice and put onto plate.
- Put curry onto plate.
- Take yoghurt and cucumber mix from fridge and put some on side of plate.
- Slice tomatoes and add to side of plate.
- Put a handful of raisins on side of plate (optional).

And wow, you just made a delicious curry! Enjoy!

Hot tip: The yoghurt and cucumber mix will take some heat out of curry, as will the yoghurt in the curry.

RECIPE 20:

Bombay surprise!

A cautionary tail

Some years ago I held a party in my home. One particular friend reckoned he could eat anything. I happened to have a small chili plant growing, with some very small chilies on it. I removed some, cut them up and offered them to him as a side dish. He grabbed a few, crammed them into his mouth, and chewed and swallowed. His face went bright red and sweat broke out in beads. Not to be outdone, he grabbed the rest. It required a number of beers to cool him down, but his verdict was that they were 'splendid'.

After three or four pints, nature took its course and he retired to 'restore his comfort'. The resultant screams brought the party to a standstill: I had forgotten to warn him to wash his hands BEFORE making himself comfortable!

Objective: To create a really hot side dish for curry without chili injuries.

Hot tip: Wash your hands really well immediately after touching chillies!

If you cook my chicken curry for a number of people, you are duty bound to make it mild to make it palatable for everyone. If you like a hot curry, however, the addition of 'Bombay surprise' will add a little zing for those who like a good glow! (The surprise lies in the fact that some people will actually eat it!)

Organisation

Gather equipment – wok or frying pan, ovenproof dish, spatula, clean tea towel, large bowl for rubbish.

Gather ingredients – medium-sized potatoes, a medium to large onion, a handful of sultanas **(optional)**, 2 red or green chillies.

Preparation

- Put bowl of hot soapy water in the sink and a clean towel nearby.

- Wash and dry hands thoroughly.
- Check worktop is clean and clear.
- Ensure tray is in place on worktop.
- Put a large bowl nearby for rubbish.
- Place equipment on the worktop close to the tray.
- Place ingredients on the worktop close to the tray.

Execution (remember to put all rubbish in the large bowl)

- Wash and dry hands thoroughly.
- Prick and microwave the potatoes until cooked and then put in the oven to crisp up for about 20 minutes.
- Remove, allow to cool, quarter and remove contents of skins keeping the potato quarters as intact as possible. Cut into half-inch cubes and put to one side.
- Top, tail, skin and finely chop the onion and put to one side.
- Wash a good handful of sultanas and put to one side **(optional)**.
- Take the chillies. Remove the top. Slice very finely, being sure to retain the seeds, and put to one side.

- NOW WASH YOUR HANDS AND DO NOT EVEN THINK OF TOUCHING ANYTHING UNTIL YOU HAVE DONE SO. YOU HAVE BEEN WARNED!
- Put a splash of oil into the wok or frying pan, bring to heat and add chopped chillies. Allow to simmer for a couple of minutes. It's a good idea to have the kitchen window open.
- Add chopped potatoes and keep turning, gently so as not to crush them. After 5 minutes add onion, mix in well, and keep turning.
- After another 5 minutes add the sultanas, and keep turning (optional).
- After 5 minutes put into ovenproof dish and put in the oven for 15 minutes.
- Put bowls or plates to warm in oven for a couple of minutes.
- Remove from the oven and serve as a side dish to the curry, rice and cucumber-yoghurt mix.

There you have it, Bombay surprise! It should make most peoples' eyes water!

NOTES

CATCH YOUR RABBIT #7

Very quick veggie meals
(easy)

RECIPE 21:

Very quick veggie meal 1

This meal is really quick and a good example of what I call 'rough cooking'. I literally sling some food together in the oven and cook it for 30 minutes. The result is surprisingly good.

Objective: To prepare a quick and easy vegetarian supper.

> **Hot tip 1:** You can skip the wok or frying pan bit if you wish (as per the next recipe) and simply chuck all this in the ovenproof dish. Cook for 20 minutes, take out and stir and add the cheese, and put back in for 20 minutes.

> **Hot tip 2:** This dish is really great Italian-style with sliced mozzarella instead of cheddar.

*Always remember the **SLO** principles: safety, lazy person principle and organisation.*

Organisation

Gather equipment – mixing bowl, wok or frying pan, vegetable chopping board, sharp knife, ovenproof dish, clean tea towel, large bowl for rubbish.

Gather ingredients – cauliflower, a large onion, button mushrooms, half a stick of celery, tin of chopped tomatoes, cheese, oil for frying, curry paste, salt and pepper.

Preparation

- Put bowl of hot soapy water in the sink and a clean towel nearby.
- Wash and dry hands thoroughly.
- Check worktop is clean and clear.
- Ensure tray is in place on worktop.
- Put a large bowl nearby for rubbish.
- Place equipment on the worktop close to the tray.
- Place ingredients on the worktop close to the tray.

Execution (remember to put all rubbish in the large bowl)

- Preheat oven to 170 degrees or gas mark 3.
- Wash and dry hands thoroughly.
- Break off florets from half of a small cauliflower and put in the bowl.
- Top, tail and skin and roughly chop a large onion.
- Put a small splash of oil into wok or frying pan and bring up to heat.
- Put onions in wok or frying pan and keep turning to get them well coated.
- Add a teaspoon of curry paste, keep turning, and after a couple of minutes add cauliflower.
- Keep turning and then reduce heat and add whole baby button mushrooms and half a stick of celery chopped up small.
- Keep turning, then add a tin of chopped tomatoes and allow to simmer for 5 minutes.
- Tip into ovenproof dish and spread a handful of grated cheese over the top.
- Bung in the oven for 30 minutes.
- Put bowl or plate to warm in oven for a couple of minutes.

The result is amazingly tasty, especially with some buttered bread to dip in and mop up.

RECIPE 22:

Very quick veggie meal 2

Objective: Experimenting with veg you like and don't like.

Hot tip: Don't overthink it, just enjoy the process of experimenting!

Following the usual guidelines with respect to our SLO principles – safety, lazy person principle, and organisation – this is another quick veggie dish.

Organisation

Gather equipment – vegetable chopping board, sharp knife, ovenproof dish, clean tea towel, large bowl for rubbish.

Gather ingredients – a leek, 6 asparagus stalks (which used to be called sparrow grass!), a courgette, a tin of chopped tomatoes – or anything else you wish to add – and a little oil, mixed herbs, salt and pepper.

Execution (remember to put all the rubbish in the large bowl)

- Wash and dry your hands thoroughly.
- Chop the bottom inch and the top three inches off a leek and slice into one-inch pieces and put in the ovenproof dish.
- Chop the bottom off the asparagus stalks and put on top of the leek.
- Top and tail a courgette, chop into one-inch pieces and put on top of the asparagus.
- Pour a tin of tomatoes over the top (grated cheese or sliced mozzarella is optional).
- Sprinkle with mixed herbs and add salt and pepper.
- Cook in the preheated oven for 30 minutes.
- Put bowl or plate to warm in oven for a couple of minutes.

Great with bread and butter and a cup of tea!

RECIPE 23:

Very quick veggie meal 3

Objective: Playing around with more veggies for a quick supper.

Hot tip: Slicing and soaking the
aubergines in salted water for
half an hour, or slicing them
and sprinkling with salt for 20
minutes, and then rinsing and
patting dry with kitchen paper
gives them a really nice flavour.

*Following the usual guidelines with respect to our **SLO** principles – **safety, lazy person principle, and organisation** – this is another quick veggie dish:*

Organisation

Gather equipment – vegetable chopping board, sharp knife, ovenproof dish, clean tea towel, large bowl for rubbish.

Gather ingredients – courgette, aubergine, mushrooms, 3 tomatoes, medium onion, cheese, Greek yoghurt, fresh (or dried) basil, salt and pepper.

Execution (remember to put all the rubbish in the large bowl)

- Preheat oven to 170 degrees or gas mark 3.
- Wash and dry your hands thoroughly.
- Soak the aubergines in salted water for half an hour, or slice and sprinkle with salt for 20 minutes **(optional),** rinse and pat dry. Chop aubergines into small chunks.
- Top and tail a courgette, chop into one-inch pieces.
- Slice 3 or 4 mushrooms.
- Put all the vegetables in an ovenproof dish.
- Chop three standard tomatoes into medium chunks.
- Top, tail and skin a medium onion and slice coarsely.
- Put tomatoes and onion into a liquidiser (or blender), add a couple of sprigs of fresh (or dried) basil and two dessertspoons of natural Greek yoghurt and blitz for 8 to 10 minutes.

- Pour over vegetables. Allow sauce to percolate for 10 minutes.
- Cover with cheese of your choice and put in the oven for 40 minutes.

This meal could easily be beefed up with the addition of pasta. I find it's best to cook the pasta for 10 minutes on its own before putting into the dish with the veg.

Failing that, a slice of homemade bread and a cup of tea works perfectly!

FOR THE
HOMEMADE BREAD

Sainsbury's do a range of ready-mixed bread kits. I've tried a couple just for the craic, but I do not use a bread-making machine, I just follow the instructions on the packet and mixed it by hand in a large mixing bowl – well, with a wooden spoon, otherwise I would have been picking dough out of my wedding ring forever!

I also don't bother with a bread tin. After shaping the dough into a cylinder, I simply placed it on a greased baking tin.

It made a lovely bloomer! Very easy and instant success. You couldn't ask for more!

All of the above meals are rough cooking at its best, with absolutely no finesse or pretence at all. All three meals could easily be beefed up with the addition of pasta or bread.

The only limiting factor is your imagination, and the contents of your fridge at the time, so just have fun! If it's not very nice, think about what you could do differently. The main thing to remember is that nobody has fallen off their perch because of some mismatched veg (as far as I know)!

NOTES

CATCH YOUR RABBIT #8

Using minced beef
(easy to moderate)

RECIPE 24:

Cottage pie

Objective: Experimenting with mince.

**Hot tip: Always stay mindful
and pay attention to what
you are doing.**

Note: Cottage pie is made with beef and shepherd's pie is made with lamb.

Always remember the **SLO** *principles:* **safety, lazy person principle and organisation.**

Organisation

Gather equipment – 2 mixing bowls, medium and small saucepans, sharp knife, wooden spoon, ovenproof dish, slotted spoon, small dish, clean tea towel, large bowl for rubbish.

Gather ingredients – minced beef, onion, carrots, 2 medium potatoes, cheese, egg, mushrooms, peas, butter or spread, 1 to 2 leeks, salt and pepper, red (tomato) sauce (**optional**). **Note**: Anchovy or Tabasco sauce works well with this dish, if you fancy experimenting!

Preparation

- Put bowl of hot soapy water in the sink and a clean towel nearby.
- Wash and dry hands thoroughly.
- Check worktop is clean and clear.
- Ensure tray is in place on worktop.
- Put a large bowl nearby for rubbish.
- Place equipment on the worktop close to the tray.
- Place ingredients on the worktop close to the tray.

Execution (remember to put all rubbish in the large bowl)

- Preheat oven to 170 degrees or gas mark 3.
- Wash and dry hands thoroughly.
- Prick the potatoes and put in microwave for 5 minutes for each potato. Turn potatoes over and put on high power for another 5 minutes each.

- Remove from microwave with a clean tea towel and test with sharp knife. If soft put in the oven to crisp up for about 20 minutes; if not, cook for a couple more minutes and then put into the oven to crisp up.
- Tip the minced beef from the container into the medium saucepan. (Be sure to remove the paper on the bottom of the packaging.)

Note: If there is too much mince for one person split it in half and put back in fridge in a labelled and dated sealed bag or airtight container. If you are cooking for more than one person use it all.

- Skin, halve and chop onion and drop into mince. Mix in.
- Top, tail and wash two carrots. Dice and drop into mince. Mix in.
- Put a mug of water in saucepan with mince and onion and put saucepan on moderate heat, stir occasionally. Keep on heat for about 15 minutes. (Alternatively, you can brown the onions and mince in wok or frying pan.)
- Put the peas in small saucepan, add

mug of water and bring to boil. Reduce heat and simmer for 5 minutes. Remove peas with slotted spoon and drop into mince.

- Add salt and pepper and mix.
- Remove mince from heat after 15 minutes and put to one side.
- Top, tail and wash a couple more carrots. Slice into batons. Put in small saucepan with water from peas. Bring to boil, reduce heat and simmer for 5 minutes. Remove with slotted spoon and place in small dish.
- Put gravy granules into small saucepan with water from peas and carrots. Turn heat up to high, stir and keep stirring.
- When mixture becomes thicker, remove from heat. Pour gravy into mince. Mix well.
- Remove potatoes from oven with tea towel. Put on chopping board.
- Cut in half and scoop contents into clean mixing bowl. Add butter and salt and pepper and mix until smooth.
- Beat an egg into a mug and add to mixture (optional).
- Add grated cheese and mix. Add salt and pepper to taste and mix.

- Halve the mushrooms and add to mince and mix well.
- Put mince mixture into ovenproof dish. Smooth and layer the mashed potatoes on top of the mince.
- Place in oven and cook for 20 minutes.
- Wash medium saucepan. Half fill with cold water and put on to boil.
- Top and tail 1 large or 2 small leeks, strip outer skin off, wash well and cut into inch-long sections.
- Put in boiling water, reduce heat, add carrot batons. Simmer for 5 minutes.
- Remove from saucepan and put in dish.
- Empty saucepan and melt a knob of butter in it.
- Add leeks and carrots and shake over a low heat until carrots and leeks are well coated. Do this for a couple of minutes, then turn heat off and leave leeks and carrots in saucepan.
- Remove dish from oven after 20 minutes.
- Put bowl or plate to warm in oven for a couple of minutes.
- Serve onto a plate and add carrots and leeks.

This meal benefits from red (tomato) sauce, but only if it's your thing!

RECIPE 25:

Pasta bake with mince

Objective: A variation of the previous recipe with pasta.

**Hot tip: If you have a container
for washed cutlery, make sure
the knives and forks
go in point down.**

Always remember the SLO principles: safety, lazy person principle and organisation.

Organisation

Gather equipment – large, medium and small saucepans, 2 mixing bowls, sharp knife, wooden spoon, colander, ovenproof dish, tin opener, clean tea towel, large bowl for rubbish.

Gather ingredients – minced beef, penne pasta, butter or spread, onion, aubergine, mushrooms, courgette, sweetcorn, plain flour, milk, garlic, tin of chopped tomatoes, chili (optional).

Preparation

- Put bowl of hot soapy water in the sink and a clean towel nearby.
- Wash and dry hands thoroughly.
- Check worktop is clean and clear.
- Ensure tray is in place on worktop.
- Put a large bowl nearby for rubbish.
- Place equipment on the worktop close to the tray.
- Place ingredients on the worktop close to the tray.

Execution (remember to put all rubbish in the large bowl)

- Wash and dry hands thoroughly.
- Put water in large saucepan with a drop of oil and put on heat to boil.
- When boiling, drop a mug of pasta into pan and turn down to simmer for 10 minutes (or the time specified on the packet). Stir occasionally.
- Remove from heat when cooked and drain.
- Put mince into medium saucepan.

- Top, tail, wash, halve and cut courgettes into eight batons. Put into a dish.
- Top, tail and skin onion. Halve and chop all the onion and drop half into mince.
- Add a mug of water to the mince and put on moderate heat for 15 minutes. Stir occasionally. (Alternatively, you can brown the onions and mince in wok or frying pan.)
- Top and tail aubergine (it's up to you whether you slice and salt first, as mentioned before) and cut into half-inch cubes. Add to courgette batons.
- Wash and halve mushrooms and put in bowl.
- Add sweetcorn to bowl.
- Take mince off the heat. Add two teaspoons of lazy garlic and half a teaspoon of chili. Mix in well.
- Preheat oven to 170 degrees or gas mark 3.

Making the white sauce

- Melt a knob of butter in small saucepan and drop in remainder of chopped onion. Keep stirring with wooden spoon.
- Remove from heat and drop a level

tablespoon of plain flour into butter. Stir in and return to heat. Stir for a couple of minutes.

- Pour in a little milk and stir. Once mixture thickens add more milk and stir.
- Repeat the process until you have a mixture the consistency of custard. Remove from heat.
- Drain some of the liquid from the mince. Add a handful of grated cheese and mix in.
- Put pasta back into large saucepan and add the mince and mix in.
- Add contents of mixing bowl and mix well.
- Add chopped tomatoes and mix well.
- Pour into ovenproof dish to just below the rim. Level it out.
- Put any surplus into a labelled and dated sealed bag or airtight container and freeze.
- Pour sauce from small saucepan over the contents of the ovenproof dish.
- Allow to stand for a couple of minutes so the sauce can sink into the mince.
- Finish off with a layer of grated cheese.
- Put in the oven for 30 minutes.

- Put bowl or plate to warm in oven for a couple of minutes.
- Remove and serve.

Hot tip: If you are only cooking for one person use your eating dish as an ovenproof dish, it saves on washing up. But be careful to let it cool as it will be super-hot when you take it out of the oven.

RECIPE 26:

Pasties: plain, chili, garlic, curry, or mixed herb

Objective: Experimenting with pastry, flavours and favourites. (We'll be exploring pastry a bit more in the next section.)

Hot tip 1: Use a very sharp knife for a clean edge when cutting pastry (but not your fingers!).

Hot tip 2: Handle the pastry as little as possible!

*Always remember the **SLO** principles: safety, lazy person principle and organisation.*

Organisation

Gather ingredients – Sainsbury's ready-rolled shortcrust or puffed pastry, minced beef, onion, carrot, potato, mixed herbs, gravy granules, curry paste, or chili, or garlic, or none of them, oil, salt and pepper.

Gather equipment – medium saucepan, wok or frying pan, 3 small dishes, sharp knife, wooden spoon and spatula, clean tea towel, large bowl for rubbish.

Preparation

- Put bowl of hot soapy water in the sink and a clean towel nearby.
- Wash and dry hands thoroughly.
- Check worktop is clean and clear.
- Ensure tray is in place on worktop.
- Put a large bowl nearby for rubbish.
- Place equipment on the worktop close to the tray.
- Place ingredients on the worktop close to the tray.

Execution (remember to put all rubbish in the large bowl)

- Preheat oven to 170 degrees or gas mark 3.
- Wash and dry hands thoroughly.
- Prick potato and put in microwave on high power for 5 minutes.
- Remove, turn over and cook for another 5 minutes.

- When cooked, remove and put in oven to crisp up for about 20 minutes.
- Top, tail and skin onion. Halve and chop. Put in small dish.
- Top, tail and wash carrots. Cut into batons and dice. Put in small dish.
- Put some water on to boil in medium saucepan. Once boiling, drop in dessertspoon of gravy granules. Keep on heat and stir vigorously. When mixture thickens remove from heat and put to one side.
- Put oil into wok or frying pan and bring to heat.
- Once hot add onions, then turn down heat and simmer for a couple of minutes (do not burn them).
- Add mince, mix in well, and keep turning for about 10 minutes on moderate heat.

Optional

Remove from heat and add mixed herbs, or two teaspoons of lazy garlic, or one teaspoon of curry paste, or half a teaspoon of chili, or none of the above. Leave to stand.

To continue

- Remove potatoes from oven with clean tea towel and put on chopping board.
- Quarter the potatoes and carefully remove contents of skins, keeping them as intact as possible. Leave potato to cool on chopping board.
- Warm gravy and pour onto mince, mix in well and add salt and pepper to taste.
- Add carrots. Mix in well.
- Remove chopping board with potato on and put to one side.
- Clean and dry work tray.
- Dust lightly with plain flour.
- Unwrap pastry and lay on tray. Use a side plate as a template and cut circles of pastry. Remove circles of pastry and carefully put to one side.
- Chop potato into quarter-inch cubes and add to mince. Mix in well.
- Take baking tray, line with foil, and place in work tray.
- Take first pastry circle and put in baking tray. (Remember you have to fold the circle in half to make a pasty.)
- Put some of the mince mixture onto one half of the pastry circle, heaped quite

high in the middle and tapering down to the edges. Leave a quarter-inch edge of bare pastry around the filling on filled side.

- Fold the other half over the mince to match up with the other side. (It may take a couple of goes to get this right!)
- When you have it placed to your satisfaction, brush milk onto edge of pastry on filled side, and press the two edges with a fork.
- Brush pasty with either beaten egg or milk. **Note**: Brushing the pasties with beaten egg once gives them a lovely gloss; taking them out halfway and brushing them again gives them a wonderful gloss; taking them out and brushing them a third time gives them a mirror finish!
- Repeat process for other circles.
- Put in preheated oven for 30 minutes.
- Put bowl or plate to warm in oven for a couple of minutes.

You can eat the pasties as they are with your fingers – when they've cooled that is! – or you can have them as part of a proper meal. If so, prepare some vegetables to go with the pasty. I suggest peas and carrots, perhaps with a baked potato if you're really hungry. You know how to do that now, so get on with it! You may also want some gravy and, again, you know how to do that, so get making some gravy!

Think for yourself and enjoy the meal!

NOTES

CATCH YOUR RABBIT #9

Pastry dishes
(moderate)

RECIPE 27:

Quiche-type flan

Objective: Experimenting with shortcrust pastry.

Hot tip: Shut cupboard doors immediately after taking something out = no black eyes or split heads!

*Always remember the **SLO** principles: **safety, lazy person principle and organisation.***

Organisation

Gather equipment – 2 mixing bowls, ovenproof dish, sharp knife, fork, 2 small dishes, foil, clean tea towel, large bowl for rubbish.

Gather ingredients – Sainsbury's ready-rolled shortcrust pastry, 3 eggs, 5 handfuls of grated cheese, half a mug of milk, medium onion, 12 button mushrooms, 8 asparagus tips, 2 tomatoes, mixed herbs

179

and salt and pepper.

Preparation

- Put bowl of hot soapy water in the sink and a clean towel nearby.
- Wash and dry hands thoroughly.
- Check worktop is clean and clear.
- Ensure tray is in place on worktop.
- Put a large bowl nearby for rubbish.
- Place equipment on the worktop close to the tray.
- Place ingredients on the worktop close to the tray.

Execution (remember to put all rubbish in the large bowl)

- Preheat oven to 170 degrees or gas mark 3.
- Wash and dry hands thoroughly.
- Unwrap the shortcrust pastry.
- Wash and dry hands again.
- Grease the bottom and insides of the ovenproof dish with a butter wrapper.
- Put the pastry into the dish and press gently into the sides. Trim the pastry leaving a slight lip standing proud of

the edges of the dish.
- Top, tail, skin and halve the onion. Slice thinly and put in small dish.
- Wash and slice mushrooms and place in a small dish.
- Put a good layer of grated cheese into the bottom of the pastry case.
- Dust the cheese with mixed herbs.
- Lay a layer of sliced onions on the cheese.
- Put another layer of cheese on to cover onions.
- Dust with mixed herbs.
- Layer the sliced mushrooms on the cheese. Cover the mushrooms with cheese.
- Put asparagus on the cheese with the tips to the middle. Form a star with end of the stalks against the side of the dish. Cover with cheese.
- Put three eggs into mixing bowl – not a colander! – and beat well with fork.
- Add a little milk and beat well. Add salt and pepper to taste and beat well.
- Gently pour the egg and milk over the contents of the dish. Make sure it covers the whole dish. Be careful to pour from the outside in to the middle. (Use your

thumb as a guide to the edge of the dish.)

- Leave for 10 minutes to allow egg and milk to percolate into the entire dish.
- Thinly slice the two tomatoes and layer on the top. (You might need 3 tomatoes, it depends on their size.)
- Put dish in oven for 30 minutes.
- Put bowl or plate to warm in oven for a couple of minutes.

You can eat this quiche-type flan either cold with a salad, or hot with new potatoes tossed in butter and green beans. The new potatoes take about 20 minutes to cook in simmering water. The green beans – don't forget to top and tail and wash them – take about 10 minutes.

RECIPE 28:

Apple, onion, walnut and stilton savoury pie

Objective: Learning to use puff pastry.

Hot tip: Stay alert. The kitchen is no place to daydream.

Always remember the **SLO** *principles:* **safety, lazy person principle and organisation.**

Organisation

Gather equipment – pie dish, large and small saucepan, chopping board, sharp knife, mixing bowl, wooden spoon, foil, slotted spoon, clean tea towel, large bowl for rubbish.

Gather ingredients – Sainsbury's ready-rolled puff pastry, 2 medium cooking apples, 2 medium onions, chili, walnut pieces, 6 ounces (approximately) of Shropshire blue cheese or stilton, salt and pepper.

Preparation

- Put bowl of hot soapy water in the sink and a clean towel nearby.
- Wash and dry hands thoroughly.
- Check worktop is clean and clear.
- Ensure tray is in place on worktop.
- Put a large bowl nearby for rubbish.
- Place equipment on the worktop close to the tray.
- Place ingredients on the worktop close to the tray.

Execution (remember to put all rubbish in the large bowl)

- Preheat oven to 170 degrees or gas mark 3.
- Wash and dry hands thoroughly.
- Unwrap the pastry and put to one side.
- Wash and dry hands again.
- Grease bottom and sides of ovenproof dish and put pastry in place, pressing gently into sides.
- Trim pastry and put trimmings to one side.
- Roll a big length of foil into a sausage-shaped tube and place in ovenproof

dish. Put ovenproof dish in the oven to blind bake for 10 minutes.
- Remove dish from oven and put to one side. Remove the foil.
- Wash and peel both apples. This is difficult if you cannot see. One method is to cut the apples into quarters, remove the core and then remove the peel with a sharp knife.
- Slice or chop the peeled apples and put in large saucepan.
- Put peel and core in the small saucepan, add mug of water, bring to boil and boil for 5 minutes. Turn off heat and put saucepan aside.
- Top, tail and skin and chop onions.
- Add the onions to the apple, then strain and add water from the small saucepan. Put on a moderate heat and keep stirring frequently.
- After 5 minutes put on low heat for 10 minutes, stirring occasionally.
- Remove from heat and put aside to stand for 10 minutes.
- Add quarter of a teaspoon of chili **(optional)** to onions and apple. Mix in well, and add salt and pepper and mix again.

- Put contents of large saucepan into pastry case in ovenproof dish with slotted spoon. Level and add layer of walnut pieces.
- Slice the cheese thinly and layer on top of the walnut pieces.
- Take the remaining pastry and cover the dish, making two slots in the middle with a knife.
- Brush milk on the edges of the pastry and press the base and the lip of the pie together on the sides of the dish.
- Brush the top with milk or beaten egg.
- Place in oven for 25 minutes.
- Put bowl or plate to warm in oven for a couple of minutes (if eating hot).

This is great cold with salad, or hot with new potatoes (wash and boil in saucepan for 15 to 20 minutes), green beans (top and tail and wash and boil in pan for 10 minutes) and lemon cabbage (coming up!).

RECIPE 29:

Lemon cabbage

*Remembering the **SLO** principles: **safety, lazy person principle and organisation:***

- Remove the outer leaves of a small white cabbage. Chop off a good-sized chunk of the cabbage and slice quite finely and put in medium saucepan with water. Bring to boil then simmer for 10 minutes.
- Meanwhile, make a basic white sauce in small saucepan using the method we've used a few times now in this book.
- Take a lemon, cut a slit in the skin and squeeze juice out (doing it this way prevents pips coming out).
- Mix well and put back to heat, stirring continually.
- After a couple of minutes remove from heat.
- Drain cabbage and add to the lemon sauce.
- Add salt and pepper.
- Simmer for 5 minutes, stirring all the time, and then remove from heat.

Serve immediately with the hot pie, new potatoes and green beans; or, alternatively, you can reheat in the saucepan when it's time to serve up.

NOTES

CATCH YOUR RABBIT #10

Fish dishes
(easy to moderate)

RECIPE 30:

Salmon fillet, new potatoes and green beans with onion sauce (optional).

Objective: A lightweight healthy meal as an alternative to all the pasta and pastry!

Hot tip: When using the hob, be very conscious of the hot spots.

*Remembering the **SLO** principles: **safety, lazy person principle and organisation.***

Note: I prefer this meal without the onion sauce, but you might like it with.

Organisation

Gather equipment – wok or frying pan, medium and large saucepans, sharp knife, wooden spatula, butter knife, ovenproof dish with lid (or use foil), colander, slotted spoon, side plate, clean tea towel, large bowl for rubbish.

Gather ingredients – salmon fillet, new

potatoes, green beans. Small onion, butter, plain flour, milk **(optional)**.

Preparation

- Put bowl of hot soapy water in the sink and a clean towel nearby.
- Wash and dry hands thoroughly.
- Check worktop is clean and clear.
- Ensure tray is in place on worktop.
- Put a large bowl nearby for rubbish.
- Place equipment on the worktop close to the tray.
- Place ingredients on the worktop close to the tray.

Execution (remember to put all rubbish in the large bowl)

- Preheat oven to 170 degrees mark 3.
- Wash and dry hands thoroughly.
- Half fill saucepans with water and put on hob on moderate heat.

To make the onion sauce (takes about 15 minutes and is optional)

- Top, tail, halve and chop small onion.

- Put butter in small saucepan and melt.
- Drop onion into the butter and simmer for a minute or so.
- Add a level tablespoon of plain flour into butter and mix. Stir for a couple of minutes, then add a little milk. Stir until it thickens then put more milk in.
- Repeat the process until the sauce has the consistency of custard, and keep on low heat and stir constantly for 10 minutes.
- Take off heat and allow to rest.
- When rest of meal is ready quickly reheat and serve.

Without the onion sauce

- Top and tail green beans, wash and put in colander.
- Wash new potatoes.
- Bring large saucepan to boil and put potatoes in, then reduce heat and simmer for 15 to 20 minutes.
- When cooked – test with the point of a sharp knife to see if soft – drain, put butter into large saucepan, allow to melt, then return potatoes and toss in the butter.

- Remove with slotted spoon and put in ovenproof dish. Turn off oven and place dish in oven with lid on (or covered with foil) to keep potatoes warm.
- Bring a small saucepan of water to boil, drop green beans in, reduce heat and simmer for 10 minutes.
- Use a slotted spoon to remove from the pan and put in ovenproof dish with the potatoes to keep warm.
- Put bowl or plate and a side plate in oven to keep warm.
- Put wok or frying pan on high heat with a little oil.
- Place the salmon fillet in pan skin side down and allow to sear for 2 to 3 minutes.
- Reduce heat to moderate and use spatula to turn fillet over.
- Put a plate and side plate in oven to warm.
- Leave for about half a minute, remove from pan and put on warmed side plate.
- Take eating bowl or plate, lay green beans down to form a bed or raft.
- Place salmon fillet on beans. Add buttered new potatoes.
- Quickly reheat onion sauce if you made

some and pour over.

Eat!

RECIPE 31:

A basic fish pie

Objective: Learning to prepare and construct a slightly more challenging meal, which I've broken down into smaller sections.

Hot tip: If using fresh fish, double-check for bones.

Remembering the SLO principles: safety, lazy person principle and organisation.

Organisation

Gather equipment – medium saucepan, ovenproof dish, sharp knife, mixing bowl, 2 chopping boards (one for fish and one for vegetables), clean tea towel, large bowl for rubbish.

Gather ingredients – fish fillets (cod, coley or hake), 2 or 3 medium-sized potatoes, peas, sweetcorn, tin of chopped tomatoes, onion, fish stock cube, butter, egg, salt and pepper.

Preparation

- Put bowl of hot soapy water in the sink and a clean towel nearby.
- Wash and dry hands thoroughly.
- Check worktop is clean and clear.
- Ensure tray is in place on worktop.
- Put a large bowl nearby for rubbish.
- Place equipment on the worktop close to the tray.
- Place ingredients on the worktop close to the tray.

Execution (remember to put all rubbish in the large bowl)

- Preheat oven to 170 degrees or gas mark 3.
- Wash and dry hands thoroughly.
- Put fish chopping board in work tray.
- Remove fish flesh from the skin. Put skins into small saucepan.
- Put fish flesh into ovenproof dish (try to cover the whole of the bottom of the dish) and dust with salt and pepper.
- Wash and dry hands thoroughly.
- Prick the potatoes and put in microwave for 5 minutes each potato. Turn potatoes

over and put on high power for another 5 minutes each.

- Remove from microwave with a clean tea towel and test with sharp knife. If soft put in the oven to crisp up; if not, cook for a couple more minutes and then put into the oven to crisp up for about 20 minutes.

To make the sauce

- Top, tail and skin medium onion. Halve and chop and put some in small saucepan with fish skins.
- Half fill saucepan with water and crumble fish stock cube into water.
- Allow to boil for 5 minutes, then turn down heat to moderate and simmer for 10 minutes.
- Put butter into medium saucepan to melt. Add most of the onion, simmer for a couple of minutes, then stir and add level tablespoon of plain flour. Stir in well and remove from heat.
- Remove fish skins from small saucepan.
- Pour a little of the liquid into butter, plain flour and onion mix. Stir and return to heat.

- When mixture thickens add more liquid and keep stirring. Repeat this until you have a sauce the consistency of custard.
- Drop in half a handful of sweetcorn and peas and mix in well. Remove from heat and put aside.
- Tip tin of chopped tomatoes over fish, level, and pour on sauce with sweetcorn and peas.

And back to the potatoes

- Take potatoes from oven, cut in half lengthways and scoop potato into mixing bowl.
- Add butter and salt and pepper and mash the potatoes.
- Add a beaten egg and half a handful of cheese and beat into the mash.
- Spread the mash over the fish, tomatoes and sauce.
- Put in oven for 15 minutes.

Add a bit of veg

- Top, tail and skin leeks, then wash and cut into one-inch lengths. Put in large saucepan.

- Top, tail and wash carrots. Cut carrots into batons and put in with leeks.
- Cover with water and put on to boil.
- Reduce heat and simmer for 10 minutes.
- Put bowl or plate to warm in oven for a couple of minutes
- Drain veg and serve with fish pie.

Hot tip: Fish cooks very quickly!

RECIPE 32:

Garlic prawn tagliatelle

Objective: Getting creative with prawns and pasta!

> **Hot tip: If the oil in the wok or frying pan catches fire do not panic. Remove from heat keeping wok or frying pan at arm's length. Put on chopping board and cover with lid. If no lid, wet a tea towel and lay over the flames. No need for drama.**

*Always remember the **SLO** principles: **safety, lazy person principle and organisation.** Getting bored with being told this? A&E is far more boring!*

Note on quantity: I usually allow two of the pasta balls for each person and one for the pot. Thus for one person allow three balls, for two people allow five balls, and so on.

Organisation

Gather equipment – large, medium and small saucepans, wok or frying pan, small dish, sharp knife, wooden spoon and spatula, clean tea towel, large bowl for rubbish.

Gather ingredients – tagliatelle, king prawns, lazy garlic, milk, plain flour, butter, button mushrooms, asparagus, peas and sweetcorn, baby plum tomatoes.

Preparation

- Put bowl of hot soapy water in the sink and a clean towel nearby.
- Wash and dry hands thoroughly.
- Check worktop is clean and clear.
- Ensure tray is in place on worktop.
- Put a large bowl nearby for rubbish.
- Place equipment on the worktop close to the tray.
- Place ingredients on the worktop close to the tray.

Execution (remember to put all rubbish in the large bowl)

- Wash and dry hands thoroughly.
- Half fill large saucepan and put on hob to boil. Add a drop of oil to the water.
- When boiling, drop tagliatelle balls into the water and reduce heat to simmer. Simmer for 10 minutes (or however long it says on the packet).
- Drain pasta in colander and put to one side.

Now for the prawns and veg

- Put some butter in the small saucepan, melt, and add a teaspoon of lazy garlic. Allow to simmer for a couple of minutes and stir to prevent burning.
- Remove from heat. Add prawns and toss in the garlic butter. Put saucepan aside.
- Halve button mushrooms.
- Cut ends off asparagus stalks and cut into one-inch lengths.
- Put asparagus tips and half a handful of sweetcorn and peas into large saucepan, cover with water and put onto boil.

Once boiling, reduce heat and simmer for no longer than a minute.
- Remove from heat and put to one side.

And then the sauce

- Put butter in medium saucepan to melt.
- Add half a teaspoon of lazy garlic, mix in, and add a level tablespoon of plain flour. Mix and put on heat.
- Add a little milk and stir until mixture thickens, then add some of the liquid from the large saucepan and stir until mixture thickens again.
- Add the rest of the liquid from the large saucepan. Stir well over the heat for about 5 minutes.
- Add peas, sweetcorn, asparagus and mix in well.
- Take off heat after a couple of minutes and add prawns. Mix in well and do not return to heat.
- Put some more water in the large saucepan and bring to boil. Drop the pasta into the boiling water, then remove from heat and leave for half a minute. Drain.
- Put bowl or plate to warm in oven for a

couple of minutes.
- Put sauce on the heat again, stirring all the time. After half a minute remove from heat and pour over pasta.

Serve and eat!

Hot tip: Prawns need only a minute of cooking otherwise they go rubbery. Less is always better.

NOTES

CATCH YOUR RABBIT #11

Slow cooker meals
(easy to moderate)

RECIPE 33:

A simple chicken stew

Objective: Having a great meal ready for you if you're going to be out all day.

Hot tip: Raw chicken is funny stuff. Hygiene is extremely important. Always use separate chopping boards for meat, fish and vegetables.

*Remembering the **SLO** principles: **safety, lazy person principle and organisation.***

Note on slow cookers: Slow cookers are great if you are going to be out for the day, as you'll have a delicious meal ready for when you get home. My slow cooker has an analogue knob. From left to right it has four settings: off, low, high, medium. Check the settings on your slow cooker. If you put it on medium to begin with you may have to wait forever for your food!

Organisation

Gather equipment – slow cooker, 2 chopping boards for meat and vegetables, 2 sharp knives, small saucepan, clean tea towel, large bowl for rubbish.

Gather ingredients – chicken pieces, onions, leeks, carrots, peas, sweetcorn, mushrooms, lazy garlic, chicken stock cube or stock pot, half a glass of red wine, paprika, Greek yoghurt.

Preparation

- Put bowl of hot soapy water in the sink and a clean towel nearby.
- Wash and dry hands thoroughly.
- Check worktop is clean and clear.
- Ensure tray is in place on worktop.
- Put a large bowl nearby for rubbish.
- Place equipment on the worktop close to the tray.
- Place ingredients on the worktop close to the tray.

Execution (remember to put all rubbish in the large bowl)

- Wash and dry hands thoroughly.
- Take chicken pieces and dice into finger-sized pieces and put into slow cooker. Put meat chopping board and meat knife to one side.
- Wash and dry hands thoroughly
- Put vegetable chopping board and new knife into work tray.
- Top, tail and skin onion, halve and slice. Put into slow cooker.
- Top, tail and wash a couple of carrots, dice and put into slow cooker.

Either: Put small saucepan on the heat with a little water and crumble chicken stock cube into water. Bring to boil and allow simmer for a couple of minutes. Remove from heat and pour liquid into slow cooker.

Or: Empty chicken stock pot into slow cooker.

- Add teaspoon of lazy garlic and glass of red wine to slow cooker.

- Put the lid on the slow cooker and turn to high. When it starts to boil (and lid starts to lift) reduce heat to medium.
- **Leave on medium for 6 hours.**
- Clear up the kitchen for your return home.

When you get home, it's time for the final part of the cooking:

- Wash and dry hands thoroughly.
- Give the slow cooker contents a stir, add button mushrooms, peas and sweetcorn, and leave for another hour.
- Top up liquid if really necessary, but it shouldn't be.
- Preheat oven to 170 degrees or gas mark 3.
- While the chicken stew is cooking for its final hour, prick and put medium-sized potatoes into microwave for as long as it takes to cook them until soft.
- Crisp potatoes in oven for about 20 minutes.
- Halve the potatoes and scoop contents into bowl and mash with butter and salt and pepper.
- Remove lid of slow cooker, add half a

tub of Greek yoghurt, dust with paprika, mix and leave to stand for a couple of minutes.

- Put bowl or plate to warm in oven for a couple of minutes.

Serve this delicious chicken stew with the mash. The perfect end to a busy day.

RECIPE 34:

Steak and kidney crumble

Objective: A bit more practice with flour to make a crumble (which we'll be doing again later with a pudding!).

Hot tip: Dispose of food waste regularly to avoid maggots.

*Remembering the **SLO** principles: **safety, lazy person principle and organisation.***

Organisation

Gather equipment – slow cooker, mixing bowl, wok or frying pan, knife, spatula, wooden spoon, slotted spoon, ovenproof dish, clean tea towel, baking tray, saucer or small bowl, clean tea towel, large bowl for rubbish.

Gather ingredients – 1 pound or 450 grams of steak and kidney mix from the butcher, 2 or 3 medium potatoes, large onion, plain flour, oil, butter or spread, mixed herbs, gravy granules, salt and pepper.

Preparation

- Put bowl of hot soapy water in the sink and a clean towel nearby.
- Wash and dry hands thoroughly.
- Check worktop is clean and clear.
- Ensure tray is in place on worktop.
- Put a large bowl nearby for rubbish.
- Place equipment on the worktop close to the tray.
- Place ingredients on the worktop close to the tray.

Execution (remember to put all rubbish in the large bowl)

- Wash and dry hands thoroughly.
- Put 4 tablespoons of plain flour into the mixing bowl.
- Add a couple of teaspoons of mixed herbs and mix in well.
- Add salt and pepper and mix well.
- Put steak and kidney mix into the flour. Mix in well to make sure the meat is coated with flour.
- Put a splash of oil into the wok or frying pan, bring to high heat, and then remove from heat and drop flour-coated meat

into the oil.
- Discard the flour.
- Return to heat and turn constantly with spatula for a couple of minutes.
- Remove from heat and put meat in the slow cooker with a slotted spoon.
- Return to heat. Add a dessertspoon of gravy granules, stir, and when it thickens add a little water.
- Keep stirring and add water until you have gravy the consistency of custard. Pour gravy into slow cooker.
- Top, tail, skin, halve and roughly chop onion. Add to slow cooker. Put lid on slow cooker and put it on high. When it starts boiling (and the lid starts to lift) reduce heat to medium after giving the contents a stir.
- **Leave on medium for 4 hours.**
- Clear up the kitchen for your return home.

When you return home:

- Preheat oven to 170 degrees or gas mark 3.
- Wash and dry hands thoroughly.
- Wash, prick and put potatoes into

microwave for 5 minutes each on high power. Turn and heat for another 5 minutes or until soft.
- Grease baking tray with oil or butter.
- Remove potatoes from microwave with clean tea towel and put on chopping board. Cut into quarters and allow 5 minutes to cool.
- Carefully remove the skin, brush each potato piece with oil (or put a little oil in a saucer and roll the potato pieces in it) and place on baking tray. Place in the oven on top shelf.
- Lift slow cooker lid and add mushrooms.
- Put 4 heaped serving spoons of plain flour into a clean bowl and add cubed butter or spread.
- Wash and dry hands thoroughly.
- Mix butter or spread into the flour with hands until it resembles biscuit crumbs.
- Pour the contents of the slow cooker into ovenproof dish.
- Top with crumble mix. Leave for 30 minutes and then place in oven.
- Check the potatoes. Unstick from the tray if necessary and return to oven.
- Put the steak and kidney crumble in the oven for about 25 minutes.

Final bit

- Top, tail and wash green beans. Put into quarter-filled medium saucepan and bring to boil. Once boiling, turn down heat and simmer for 5 minutes.
- Remove from heat.
- Put bowl or plate to warm in oven for a couple of minutes.
- Remove steak and kidney crumble from oven, serve up, add roast potatoes and green beans using the slotted spoon. There should be sufficient gravy in the meal without having to make extra.

Again, this is such a nourishing, comforting meal to return to if you've been out for hours. And even you haven't been out, it's great knowing it's slowly cooking away for when you're ready to eat it.

Hot tip: You can have either roast potatoes or a baked potato with this dish.

RECIPE 35:

A delicious vegetable stew

Objective: to continue the process of being creative.

Hot tip: Feel and smell vegetables, and any doubts about freshness do not use.

*Remembering the **SLO** principles: **safety, lazy person principle and organisation.***

Organisation

Gather equipment – slow cooker, sharp knife, potato peeler, serving spoon, clean tea towel, large bowl for rubbish.

Gather ingredients – leeks, large potato, carrots, new potatoes, pearl barley, sweet potato, bell pepper, parsnip, garlic cloves, cauliflower, celery, sweetcorn, vegetable stockpot, mixed herbs, salt and pepper.

Preparation

- Put bowl of hot soapy water in the sink and a clean towel nearby.
- Wash and dry hands thoroughly.
- Check worktop is clean and clear.
- Ensure tray is in place on worktop.
- Put a large bowl nearby for rubbish.
- Place equipment on the worktop close to the tray.
- Place ingredients on the worktop close to the tray.

Execution (remember to put all rubbish in the large bowl)

- Wash and dry hands thoroughly.
- Wash 2 medium sweet potatoes and peel. When you have peeled the sweet potato, wash and dry. Feel the potato to see if you removed all the skin – the skin will be drier than the underlying flesh. Dice into half-inch cubes and put into slow cooker.
- Sprinkle a little pearl barley over the sweet potato.
- Top, tail and wash 2 or 3 carrots, slice and put in the slow cooker.

- Put a layer of new potatoes on top of the carrots and sprinkle some mixed herbs over.
- Top, tail, skin and slice 2 small or one large onion.
- Top, tail, wash 2 parsnips and cut into batons. Add to slow cooker.
- Top, tail and remove outer skin of two leeks. Wash, cut into half-inch lengths and put in slow cooker.
- Sprinkle on more pearl barley.
- Add a small tin of sweetcorn or handful of frozen sweetcorn **(optional)**.
- Take half a stick of celery, wash, and cut into small batons and add to slow cooker.
- Top, tail and skin 3 garlic cloves, slice lengthways and sprinkle over the celery.
- Take a quarter of a small cauliflower, break off individual florets and sprinkle on celery and garlic. The smaller leaves can be added to the cooker. The stalk can also be chopped up small and added.
- Add the contents of a vegetable stockpot.
- Add half a glass of white wine.
- Put lid on the slow cooker turn up high. When it comes to the boil (and the lid

starts jumping) reduce heat to medium.
- **After 2 or 3 hours, if you're home, add another half a glass of wine.**
- **After 5 or 6 hours turn the slow cooker down to low.**
- Clear up the kitchen.

When it's soon time to eat:

- Preheat oven to 170 degrees or gas mark 3.
- Wash and dry hands thoroughly.
- Wash and pierce large potato and put in the microwave for 5 minutes. Turn and cook for 5 minutes more.
- Test and if soft put in the oven to crisp up for about 20 minutes. Decide if you are going to have a baked potato or mashed potatoes.
- Remove the lid of the slow cooker and give the stew a good stir. Add salt and pepper (if needed) and stir again. Return lid and turn up to hot.
- Put bowl or plate to warm in oven for a couple of minutes.
- Prepare the potato for either mash or baked, and put on plate. Add a good helping of vegetable stew.

Note: You can keep a stew like this going for a few days just by adding more vegetables and vegetable stock as required. It's ideal for cold winter evenings, and with a soft roll to mop up the gravy it can be a really warming and filling feast. And don't be afraid to experiment with the ingredients. Leave out the things you don't like, and add the things you do.

Hot tip: Do not allow the stew to dry out when reheating.

NOTES

CATCH YOUR RABBIT #12

The full roast!
(challenging, but so satisfying!)

RECIPE 36:

A full roast chicken lunch or dinner (serves four)

Objective: To learn to cook and time many things to create a perfect roast dinner (and not to panic!).

Note: At first glance, cooking this meal must look like a nightmare. It is, however, quite simple. All it requires is timing, so read the instructions a couple of times and then get stuck in. There is nothing here that is beyond you, and is only a combination of the things we have practiced from this book many times.

Hot tip: Do not rush, think logically, and stay calm and focussed.

Remembering the **SLO** *principles:* **safety, lazy person principle and organisation.** *You can do this!*

Organisation

Gather your equipment – deep oven tray or roasting tin, 2 chopping boards for meat and veg, 1 large saucepan with a lid, 2 medium saucepans and lids, colander, 2 sharp knives, 4 medium dishes, 2 mixing bowls, slotted spoon, 2 covered serving dishes or covered ovenproof dishes, small saucer or dish, butter knife, dessertspoon, large bowl for rubbish.

Gather ingredients – chicken gravy granules. Ready-mix sage and onion stuffing, mushrooms, cooking apple (all optional).

You have three options with stuffing:

- You can use it as it is and not add anything at all.
- You can add a chopped apple, or a chopped onion, or raisins to the ready-mix.
- You don't have to have any stuffing at all!

Preparation

- Put bowl of hot soapy water in the sink and a clean towel nearby.
- Wash and dry hands thoroughly.
- Check worktop is clean and clear.
- Ensure tray is in place on worktop.
- Put a large bowl nearby for rubbish.
- Place equipment on the worktop close to the tray.
- Place ingredients on the worktop close to the tray.

Execution (remember to put all rubbish in the large bowl)

- Have a cup of tea, read the instructions again, and get everything clear in your mind.
- Preheat the oven to 170 degrees or gas mark 3.
- Wash and dry your hands thoroughly.
- Wash, prick and put potatoes into microwave. Allow 5 minutes for each potato. Turn and cook for 5 minutes more or until soft.
- Put the meat chopping board in the work tray.

- Remove the packaging from the chicken, taking note of the weight. A rule of thumb is that meat requires 20 minutes per pound in weight (or 450 grams) plus 20 minutes. Therefore, a 1.9 kilogram chicken weighs roughly 4 pounds and will require 80 minutes plus 20 minutes.
- After removing the packaging, remove the elastic band from around the legs and pull legs out of the body. Put the ready-mix stuffing into the body cavity as it is. Or add one of the three additional ingredients and put into the chicken. Or don't add any stuffing at all.
- Whether you stuff the chicken or not, rub a little salt into the skin. Leave for a few minutes. Brush salt off.
- Put the chicken into the roasting dish.
- Wash the meat chopping board and meat knife thoroughly. Wash and dry hands thoroughly. This is important to prevent cross contamination!

Take a breath, and:

- Put the vegetable chopping board in the work tray.

- Remove the potatoes from the microwave with a clean tea towel and put on the chopping board. Quarter and allow to cool.
- Carefully remove skin and coat or roll the potato quarters in oil.
- Put in roasting tin with the chicken.
- Put the roasting tin with the chicken into the preheated oven. **Note**: The cooking time starts now.
- Wash and dry hands thoroughly.
- Take the parsnips, top, tail and wash. Cut into quarters lengthways. Put in a dish.
- Top, tail, wash and cut carrots into batons. Put into a dish.
- Strip the outer leaves off the Brussels sprouts and put into a dish.
- Top, tail and wash green beans and put into a dish.
- Top, tail and skin the shallots and leave on the chopping board.

At this stage everything is nicely on schedule, so relax and have a cup of tea (or a glass of wine). You've earned it!

- After about 45 minutes remove the

roasting tin and put on chopping board.
- By this time quite a lot of fat and juice will have come out of the chicken, so use a tablespoon to pour some of the juice over the chicken. This will help to crisp it up nicely.
- Take a butter knife and carefully turn the potatoes over. Pour some of the chicken juice over the potatoes.
- Return the roasting tin to the oven for another 55 minutes.
- Half fill the large saucepan and put on the heat. Bring to boil and add the parsnips. Reduce the heat and simmer for 5 minutes.
- Remove from heat, drain and rinse with cold water. Roll the parsnip batons in oil and add to the roasting tin.
- Add the shallots to the roasting tin.

At this stage you should have the chicken, potatoes, parsnips and shallots in the roasting tin. Check the time. There should be about 45 minutes to go, or thereabouts.

- Refill the large saucepan and put back on the hob.
- Once boiling, put in the carrots and the

green beans. Put the sprouts in the colander and place on the simmering saucepan to steam. Cover with saucepan lid.

- Leave the saucepan simmering for no more than 10 minutes, then remove from heat.
- Put the sprouts into a dish.
- Remove the beans and carrots with a slotted spoon and put into a dish. Keep the water for the gravy.
- Turn off the oven.
- Remove the chicken and put sprouts in the oven to keep warm.
- Cover the chicken with foil and leave it to rest, but first remove the roast potatoes and parsnips and put into a dish in the oven to keep warm.
- Tip some of the juice from the roasting tin into a medium saucepan. Add gravy granules and bring to heat, stirring briskly.
- When liquid thickens add some of the water from the carrot and bean saucepan and mix briskly.
- When it thickens again add some more liquid and stir.
- Remove from heat and put to one side.

- Very carefully carve the chicken. (It might be a good idea to ask someone else to do this if totally blind.)
- Put bowls and plates to warm in oven for a couple of minutes.
- Take everything out of the oven and put on the table.
- Put gravy in small jug or gravy boat and put on the table.

You are now ready to serve up your chicken lunch for four, and everything is hot! So what was all the fuss about?

If you have prepared one of the puddings that come next, it can cook while the roast chicken dinner is being eaten.

Any chicken left over can be used for a chicken salad the following day, and chicken mayo sandwiches the day after.

Do not reheat chicken, it is not worth the risk.

Hot tip: You can do this, so remember to breathe, relax, and enjoy it!

NOTES

CATCH YOUR RABBIT #13

Puddings
(of course!)

RECIPE 37:

Blackberry and apple crumble

Objective: Who needs an objective when it comes to puddings!

Hot tip: Wild blackberries are lovely. Do not collect near a busy road, though, and remember they have resident livestock in the form of bugs, so soak them in water with a little salt before using so the bugs vacate the blackberries!

*Remembering the **SLO** principles: **safety, lazy person principle and organisation.***

Organisation

Gather equipment – large saucepan, sharp knife, colander, ovenproof dish, mixing bowl, dessertspoon, clean tea towel, large bowl for rubbish.

Gather ingredients – blackberries, cooking apple, brown sugar, raisins **(optional)**, measure of rum or glass of sherry, plain flour, butter.

Preparation

- Put bowl of hot soapy water in the sink and a clean towel nearby.
- Wash and dry hands thoroughly.
- Check worktop is clean and clear.
- Ensure tray is in place on worktop.
- Put a large bowl nearby for rubbish.
- Place equipment on the worktop close to the tray.
- Place ingredients on the worktop close to the tray.

Execution (remember to put all rubbish in the large bowl)

- Preheat oven to 170 degrees or gas mark 3.
- Wash and dry hands thoroughly.
- Put blackberries in water with a little salt. Leave them for an hour.
- Skim any livestock off the surface of the water with a slotted spoon and put blackberries into colander. Wash thoroughly under cold water, drain and

place in large saucepan.
- Core and skin a cooking apple, slice, and put in large saucepan.
- Sprinkle one serving spoon of brown sugar onto apple and blackberries.
- Add a handful of raisins and half a mug of water and mix well **(optional)**.
- Put on moderate heat, stirring occasionally.
- When the apple is soft take off heat and stir well. Add measure of rum or glass of sherry. Leave to stand.
- Put 4 heaped serving spoons of plain flour into mixing bowl. Add quarter of block of butter (which has been out of the fridge for a while) after dicing finely. Mix into flour with a fork for a little while.
- Wash and dry hands thoroughly.
- Rub the butter into the flour until the contents of the mixing bowl resemble biscuit crumbs. Add a dessertspoon of brown sugar and mix in well.
- Put apple and blackberry mix into an ovenproof dish. Sprinkle the crumble mix over the top, making sure all the fruit is covered.
- Put in the oven for 25 minutes.

- Remove from oven and serve with cream, custard or ice cream. Enjoy!

**Hot tip: Allow fruit to steep
for at least 20 minutes
to absorb the booze!**

RECIPE 38:

Bread and butter pudding

Objective: Again, no objective required.

Hot tip: Wash any dried fruit.

*Always remember the **SLO** principles: **safety, lazy person principle and organisation.** Still fed up of reading this bit? You'll be super fed up if you end up in A&E!*

Organisation

Gather equipment – ovenproof dish, dessertspoon, butter knife, mixing bowl, fork, clean tea towel, large bowl for rubbish.

Gather ingredients – bread, butter, brown sugar, raisins, sultanas, ground cinnamon, milk, eggs.

Preparation

- Put bowl of hot soapy water in the sink and a clean towel nearby.

- Wash and dry hands thoroughly.
- Check worktop is clean and clear.
- Ensure tray is in place on worktop.
- Put a large bowl nearby for rubbish.
- Place equipment on the worktop close to the tray.
- Place ingredients on the worktop close to the tray.

Execution (remember to put all rubbish in the large bowl)

- Preheat oven to 170 degrees or gas mark 3.
- Wash and dry hands thoroughly.
- Butter 3 or 4 pieces of bread, cut into quarters and make a layer of bread and butter on the bottom of the ovenproof dish. Do not have overlaps. Any bread left over can form the next layer.
- Put a layer of sultanas and raisins on the bread and butter. Dust very lightly with ground cinnamon.
- Butter some more bread and quarter. Form another layer of bread and butter in the ovenproof dish. Sprinkle with a mixture of sultanas and raisins. Sprinkle very lightly with brown sugar.

- Make another layer of bread and butter. Sprinkle lightly with sultanas and raisins. Dust very lightly with cinnamon.
- Form another layer of bread and butter. If this layer is level with top of the dish, sprinkle very lightly with brown sugar. If not, continue layering until you are level with top of the ovenproof dish.
- Break 2 eggs into the mixing bowl, add half a mug of milk and beat with the fork for a minute or so.
- Carefully pour egg mixture over the pudding. Allow 10 minutes for it to percolate.
- Put in oven for 30 minutes.

Serve with cream, custard or ice cream.

RECIPE 39:

A traditional Royal Naval pudding (a definite health warning on this one!)

This dish is basically a 'spotted dog' (or Dick) with attitude, but a person for whom I have enormous respect thinks the name of this pudding might upset people. The name, if you wish, is a little mystery for you to solve. No doubt any ex-matelots will recognise it for what it is. Needless to say, it was a hot favourite in both the wardroom and before the mast in Nelson's ships.

Objective: To survive consumption of this pudding.

Hot tip: Keep the suet in the freezer until you're ready to use it.

*Always remember the **SLO** principles: safety, lazy person principle and organisation.*

Note: This pudding is so injurious to waistlines and arteries it seems almost hypocritical to talk about safety. However, you will have no problem with the lazy person principle after a bowl of this!

Organisation

Gather equipment – a very large saucepan, mixing bowl, cloth cotton or muslin square, 3 lengths of string, very large sturdy spoon for mixing, clean tea towel or cloth, large bowl for rubbish.

Gather ingredients – Atora suet (keep this in the freezer until ready to use), plain flour, raisins, nutmeg, cinnamon, brown sugar, milk and rum.

Preparation

- Put bowl of hot soapy water in the sink and a clean towel nearby.
- Wash and dry hands thoroughly.
- Check worktop is clean and clear.
- Ensure tray is in place on worktop.
- Put a large bowl nearby for rubbish.
- Place equipment on the worktop close

to the tray.

- Place ingredients on the worktop close to the tray.

Execution (remember to put all rubbish in the large bowl)

- Wash and dry hands thoroughly.
- Put 4 cups of plain flour into the mixing bowl.
- Add half a cup of brown sugar.
- Add 1 cup of large raisins.
- Add 2 teaspoons of nutmeg.
- Add 2 teaspoons of cinnamon.
- Mix in well with large spoon. Do not touch with hands at this stage.
- Remove the half-pound packet of Atora suet from freezer and tip into the mixing bowl. (The suet looks and feels like maggots or weevils, but do not lose heart, it works out in the end!)
- Mix well with large spoon.
- Measure three quarters of a pint of milk into a jug, and add the same amount of rum. (We used to add rum as the water on board naval ships was pretty lively and not really fit for drinking!)
- Add the milk and rum to the mixture a

small splosh at a time. First splosh and mix well.

- Second splosh and mix well.
- Third splosh and mix well.
- By this time the mixture is getting pretty stiff, and this is why you need the very large and solid spoon. (And by this time it will be starting to smell rather good too!)
- Fourth splosh and mix well.
- Add the rest and mix well.
- Keep mixing until all trace of liquid has gone.
- Put the bowl to one side.
- Wash and dry hands thoroughly.

You should by now have a fairly large shaggy beast sitting in the bowl, which you now need to wodge into a ball.

- Make sure work tray is clean and dry, then spread a layer of plain flour across the tray.
- Remove the ball of pudding mixture and place on the tray.
- Cover with a clean tea towel and leave to rest for 10 minutes. This enables all the liquid to be absorbed.

- After 10 minutes give the worktop a quick clean and dry with kitchen paper. Lightly flour the worktop and place ball of mixture onto the surface. Remove the cloth.
- You now knead the mixture for up to 20 minutes, or until it turns into an elastic dough.
- To knead the ball flatten it so that it forms a large circle. Bring the edges of the circle into the middle pressing firmly. Flatten the mixture into a circle again and repeat the procedure.
- Repeat this until the resultant dough is elastic.
- Shape the dough into a cylinder about 12 inches (or 30 centimetres) long and put it into the work tray.
- Fill very large saucepan three quarters full with water and put on to boil.
- Prepare muslin square or cotton cloth by soaking it in water and laying it across the three pieces of string, one at each end a couple of inches in and one in the middle.
- Coat the cloth with a good layer of flour. This will form a crust over the pudding.
- Lay the cylinder across the cloth and

wrap the cloth around it. Tie at each end and the middle with the string. (Use an ordinary bow so the knot will be easy to release.)

- When the water is boiling, place the muslin roll into the water, cover, reduce heat and leave to boil for two and a half hours.
- Check liquid levels occasionally. Liquid must cover the pudding.
- After two and a half hours, turn off the heat, remove the lid, and very carefully take saucepan over to the sink.
- Tip out as much water as you can (be careful not to tip out the pudding!).
- Using a tea towel or oven gloves, grab each end of the muslin-covered roll and place onto tray.
- Undo the knots and remove the cloth.

And there she is, a Royal Naval 'spotted dog' (Dick) pudding. It looks unattractive, but smells amazing, and tastes even better.

Serve with ice cream, cream or custard. Enjoy! (And then fall asleep.)

EXERCISES

Getting your hands back

When severe sight loss or blindness sets in one of the major challenges is to have confidence in where our hands are and what they are doing. (Normally we know exactly where we're placing our hands, even when we cannot see them.)

This is the sense of proprioception. There is nothing mysterious about proprioception. We have lived with it all our lives and not really noticed it. It allows us to eat, drive a vehicle, dress ourselves and put things away without really looking at what we are doing.

In order to get this sense working effectively again, I have created this series of simple exercises that do not require anything but ordinary household objects. By working on these exercises on a daily basis, if only for twenty minutes, you will be surprised how quickly your skill level will grow.

The exercises are intended for people with very little or no vision. If you find that you can still see what you are doing, then to get the most out of the exercises do them with your eyes closed. Remember, the more you practice and the less you cheat, the greater the control you will have over what your hands are doing.

There is no need to panic at the thought of these exercises. Those of you who have been in the forces will recall the ease with which you were able to strip and reassemble a rifle blindfolded. This is no different. Those who have not served, think about the last time you looked when you were engaging your seat belt. And for those who drive, how often you look at the pedals or the gear stick.

Before even thinking about trying to do any of the exercises it is important to feel calm and relaxed. We spend so much of our time flapping about, and in a state of chaos and panic, that it is difficult to know how to calm everything down to a manageable level.

So, before starting any exercise, sit in a comfortable but upright chair. Spend time moving muscles, starting with the feet and finishing with the head. This is an opportunity to really get to know your body and spend focussed time on just yourself. Let nothing distract you, this is your time. Once you feel calm and in touch with yourself, start the exercises. Be careful not to fall asleep instead when you're relaxing!

As a warm-up exercise you might find it helpful to touch your index finger to your nose. Do this a few times with each hand. Then, before moving onto the exercises, spend a couple of minutes thinking about how you were able to do that.

Then move on to these exercises, which help restore proprioception and balance.

EXERCISE ONE

- Sit comfortably in an armchair or at a table.
- Rest elbows on the arms of the chair or the table, with the forearms vertical and the fingertips of each hand pointing toward each other.
- Keeping the hands horizontal, move them toward each other until the tips of the index fingers meet. (You may find this surprisingly hard to do, so take your time until you can make them meet every time.)
- Once you have brought the index fingertips together five times in a row, rest for a few minutes and think about what you have just done. When you are ready move onto the next stage.
- Adopt the same position.
- Keeping the left hand still bring the right index fingertip to the left index finger tip. Once you have managed five successful repetitions in a row stop for a minute or so.
- Repeat, but this time bring the left index finger to the right one. After five

successful repetitions stop.

When you have completed the exercise successfully then you can safely conclude that your sense of proprioception is still alive and well, and it just needs a prod to restore your confidence in it. The important thing to remember is that you must work at the speed at which you are comfortable and not feel pressure to move onto the next exercise.

EXERCISE TWO

This exercise is to build on the work carried out in exercise one. You will need two coasters, or small mats, and one eggcup.

- Seat yourself comfortably at a table or work space.
- Place the small mats or coasters on the table within easy reach in front of you, roughly half a metre or eighteen inches apart.
- Place the eggcup on the table in front of you.
- Touch the left-hand mat with your left hand, then place the eggcup on the left-hand mat with your right hand without touching your left hand.
- Remove your right hand and place in your lap.
- Pause for a count of five.
- Collect and return the eggcup to the original position in front of you with your right hand.
- Repeat this exercise five times.
- Once happy with placing and removing the eggcup on the left-hand mat, keep

your left hand in place as a marker and place the eggcup on the right-hand mat.

- Do this for five successful repetitions.
- When satisfied you can do the exercise successfully, repeat using your left hand to move the eggcup to the right-hand mat using your right hand as a marker.
- Complete five successful repetitions.
- Repeat the exercise with your left hand to the left-hand mat.
- Complete five successful repetitions.
- Seated in the same position, then place the eggcup in front of you.
- Repeat the exercise for each hand, but this time do not use the non-active hand as a marker but place it in your lap.

Before moving onto the next exercise take a moment to think about what you have achieved. Consider how those simple movements can be used in your daily life.

EXERCISE THREE

For this exercise you need four mats or coasters, an eggcup and a table or worktop.

- Seat yourself comfortably at the table or worktop, spread the coasters in front of you in a shallow curve, with a hand's breadth between them, and number them one to four left to right in your head.
- To start, rest your left hand to the left of #1 mat. Keep your left hand where it is throughout this part of the exercise.
- Place the eggcup in the start position just in front of you and inside the curve of mats.
- With your right hand place the eggcup on #1 mat.
- Leaving the eggcup where it is, bring your right hand back to the start position.
- Pause for a count of five.
- Collect the eggcup with your right hand and return it to the start position.
- Pause for a count of five.
- Repeat the exercise for #2 mat, then

#3 mat, then #4 mat.

- Take a couple of minutes to think about the exercise, then repeat it.
- Using the same hands do exactly as you did before, but this time place the eggcup on the mats in the opposite order: #4, #3, #2, then #1.
- When you have completed this part of the exercise repeat it exactly, but with a difference: the right hand rests to the right of #4 mat and the left hand is doing the work.

When you have completed the whole exercise, you may wish to try it without a hand being used as a marker. But do not consider attempting this until you are satisfied with your performance on this exercise.

So far we have worked at one level, that is horizontally. It is also important to develop skills up and down, or vertically.

EXERCISE FOUR

This is a simple and practical exercise, but should be attempted only if you can walk easily.

- Simply walk round your home and locate the light switches. You should find that they are at a uniform height, and that many, if not all of them, will be in a consistent position with relation to the door frame.
- Then practice by finding and using just one light switch at a time.
- Once you are satisfied you can find this one switch first time every time, move on to the others.
- Continue the exercise until you are satisfied that you can find all the light switches first time every time.

As before, if you have some sight, close your eyes as you locate the switches. Despite not making much difference whether a light is on or off, if suffering from sight loss, this exercise is a lesson in 'mapping' both your house in general, and light switches specifically, thus aiding memory and coordination skills.

EXERCISE FIVE

- Go into the kitchen and stand in front of the multi-level cupboards.
- Remove some items from one of the shelves in the cupboard and put them on the worktop.
- Pause for a count of twenty.
- Put the items back on the same shelf in the same cupboard.
- Repeat for the next shelf.
- Repeat for any other shelves in the cupboard.

Work at this until you are happy you can find any shelf with ease. (This exercise is invaluable for learning your way around your kitchen when cooking.)

EXERCISE SIX

This exercise involves getting things organised, as well as using your hands to identify different objects.

- Take the cutlery out of its drawer and place it in a large bowl or container.
- Return the cutlery to the drawer piece by piece.
- Ensure each piece goes into the right compartment.
- If the cutlery drawer is not compartmentalised, then this might be a good time to do it.

So far only the hands have been used. However, one of the things that makes us stand out from nearly all other species is the use of tools.

The following exercises are designed to help you appreciate that tool-use is possible without sight. For example, this account was written on a PC without a screen or sight, which demonstrates the possibility of achieving all sorts of things.

EXERCISE SEVEN

You will need a thick piece of wood, nails and a hammer for this exercise – and ensure the nails are short enough so they will not go right through the wood. I suggest a ten-centimetre or four-inch thick piece of wood, with seven-centimetre or three-inch nails.

- Start by holding the point of the nail against the wood with the left hand (the right hand if you are left-handed).
- Gently hit the nail with the hammer.
- Continue hitting the nail gently until you feel confident you can hit it every time.
- Once the nail is lodged firmly in the wood remove the left hand and start to hit the nail more firmly.

Repeat the exercise until you have either had enough or you feel you have mastered using a hammer without sight.

EXERCISE EIGHT

For this exercise you will need some string or wool and a pair of scissors.

- Seat yourself comfortably at a table.
- Spread a newspaper or cloth in front of you to contain the mess.
- Cut short lengths off the string or wool onto the cloth or newspaper.

This is harder than it sounds. You will need to think about how to do it and, as will all things, visualise what you are doing.

EXERCISE NINE

For this you will require some dried pasta such as fusilli or macaroni, a pair of kitchen tongs and two bowls.

- Seat yourself comfortably at the table with two bowls in front of you.
- Put the dried pasta in one of the bowls.
- Using the tongs transfer the pasta from the one bowl to the other.
- Altering the distance and angle between the bowls, then transfer the pasta back.

All the above exercises help to develop both your skill and confidence in your proprioceptive sense. The last exercises also help with balance.

EXERCISE TEN

- Take a plastic jug and fill it with water to within an inch of the top.
- Find somewhere suitable and practice walking up and down with the jug of water. The objective, obviously, is not to spill any!
- Once you feel confident doing that, try going around sharp corners and up and down steps or stairs.
- Once you have mastered carrying something with one hand without spilling it, try the same exercise with a bowl of water held with both hands.

You will find this surprisingly difficult, but still achievable.

EXERCISE ELEVEN

This exercise is to help both balance and proprioception. Ideally it should be carried out whilst standing; but having seen people put their backs out just picking up a pencil, be sure to bend your knees and not your back when practising this exercise.

- Place some objects on the floor.
- Locate an item with your foot.
- Move the foot away and bend down to pick the object up.
- Repeat for all the objects.

MISCELLANEOUS EXERCISES

There are, of course, many exercises you can try to help relearn old taken-for-granted skills. One such skill could be putting a plug in a socket. This is a lot harder than you think, and the more you practice the easier it will become. The same applies to putting a key in a lock or an electric bulb in a lamp. Basically, when you come across something with which you have difficulty, put time aside to practice until it is no longer a problem.

Another skill you might find useful to learn is to use an electronic key pad. This is made easier by the number five having a little bump on it. The bump is hard to find sometimes, but it is always there. This is essential for entering numbers like PIN numbers at cash points, for example.

As you become more confident in using your hands, it may be useful to consider simple activities that still cause difficulties. As an example, after two years of sight loss I experience no difficulty in picking up a pint glass but find door handles problematic.

If you smoke, you may wish to practice lighting your cigarettes in private, on your own, before trying in public!

It may seem that many of the exercises appear tedious, trivial and dumbed down versions of real life. All I can say is that they have helped me.

An example of this is the simple operation of making a cup of tea and carrying it upstairs. To begin with it was a struggle to find a cup, put a teabag in it, fill it from the kettle, remove the teabag and locate and add milk. There would be a huge amount of thrashing about and fumbling to complete this task. Now, using my hip as a marker against the worktop and my work tray, the whole operation is carried out seamlessly. But it did not just happen, it was the product of hard work and not a little grief! And I now use a one-cup kettle, because I feel it is far safer as there is minimal risk of coming into contact with boiling water. Whilst passing through the lounge to the stairs is not without its dramas, the act of going upstairs with no sight or balance is, surprisingly, not.

There is an exercise you might like to try just for fun. It was suggested by my daughter Jaelith, so I have called it the J.A.E. or Jae's Awful Exercise! Try laying out the standard card game Patience. The hard bit is to get the columns not only straight, but also evenly spaced!

Another exercise which is useful when you start cooking again is to slice an onion. Top and tail and peel the onion first, then cut it in half and slice the halves as finely as you can manage. Use a sharp knife and use your finger as a marker. Build speed slowly, otherwise you will have bits of finger in with your onion!

I once read that a skill can be defined as 'a collection of separate operations which come together in a single smooth performance'. And in daily life, one of the operations we absolutely need to get right is the accurate use of our hands, as they are the basis for so many skills. These exercises help to re-establish confidence in their use, and are both enabling and empowering.

LAST WORD

When you're put into a position where you suddenly have to cook for yourself it can be very daunting. The degree of organisation and attention to detail that was required to cook even the most basic food was a real eye opener for me. With any luck, using this book will take away a considerable degree of alarm if you find yourself in the same position.

Whenever there is a major change of circumstances in life, we have to adjust and accept what has happened and move on. This is even more graphically illustrated if we become impaired or disabled in any way. For anyone in this situation, failure to adjust and move on invariably means staying trapped in a limbo of unfulfillable past expectations, and fresh targets cannot be generated to create mobility within the new reality.

This involves a huge amount of work, I know, if there are not to be frequent tears before bedtime, and there will be a certain amount of resistance or frustration or even anger. But nothing stays the same for long, and suddenly there is the prospect of growth and development as a person – something we were actually designed to do as evolving human beings, whatever our circumstances.

It's worth the time to take a good hard look at ourselves to try and see what is really going on when we resist something or get angry. The job, then, is to drag whatever we find within ourselves out into the open, (probably kicking and screaming!) so that we can deal with it. The choice, as I've always said, is ours.

As you've worked your way through the book you will be stunned by how many techniques you've picked up; and, in theory, you should now have moved from making a cup of tea to producing a full-blown chicken lunch or dinner for four people. But even if you have learnt just a few of these recipes, whether you are blind or not, this is an enormous step on the path to independence.

I know I keep banging the safety drum, but the safety tips are so important. They are the result of both identifying the obvious and of hard experience! The main thing is to relax, enjoy the experience and savour the amazing food you have produced.

Enjoy!

Simon Mahoney

SUMMARY OF HOT TIPS

(in no particular order)

- Regularly wash and dry your hands thoroughly, especially after handling meat or fish.

- Keep blades of knives pointing away from you.

- Always work within the confines of your work tray to prevent food or equipment escaping onto the floor!

- Have regular checks made on your equipment – the oven, hob, microwave, electric wok, kettle, for example – to make sure it is in full working order.

- Have a low rail fitted in front of hob.

- Keep separate chopping boards for meat, fish and vegetables to prevent contamination.

- Close cupboard doors and drawers

immediately.

- Turn off heat on hob between tasks.

- Dispose of food often to prevent maggots.

- Do not overthink anything, but stay mindful and focussed.

- Do not touch plugs with wet hands.

- Do not rush. Ever.

- Enjoy it, it is fun.

- Freeze any surplus food in labelled, dated airtight containers.

- Handle raw chicken carefully and wash hands immediately afterwards.

- Keep saucepan handles parallel to the worktop to prevent knocking them onto the floor.

- Heat once applied cannot be undone, so increase heat slowly so as not to burn what's in the pan.

- Keep your worktop uncluttered.

- Pasta swells half as big again when cooked.

- Prawns and fish cook very quickly.

- Prick potatoes and pierce any coverings on ready meals before putting in microwave.

- Read instructions at least twice.

- Replace tops of jars immediately, like mayonnaise, so lids don't get mixed up.

- Reverse engineer each meal; in other words, think about the end result and work backwards to see how to achieve it.

- Rice swells to twice its size when cooked.

- Put scalds and burns under cold water as quickly as possible.

- Smell ingredients, and if any doubt about freshness discard.

- Stir sauces all the time otherwise they go lumpy.

- Timing is everything, so keep practising.

- Turn food from the edges of the pan into the middle of the pan.

- Use water from vegetables for gravy, it's tastier.

- Use your imagination with ingredients! And have fun experimenting!

- Use a clean tea towel for hot ingredients like potatoes as oven gloves can get grubby.

- Use oven gloves for hot pans and oven dishes.

- Use sharp knives as blunt ones, believe it or not, cause more injuries.

- Keep a large bowl nearby for rubbish. A

mixing bowl works well.

- Listen for sizzling butter or boiling water to let you know when it's ready for cooking.

- Your sense of smell will quickly recognise when food is cooked, or burnt, which you'll learn to avoid if you don't like the taste of carbon!

- Use a digital or voice recognition timer for cooking times. Talking watches, Alexa or Siri (or other timing app) work perfectly well.

- Always remember to turn the hob and oven off when you've finished cooking.

- Warming your plates and dishes keeps food hotter for longer when completing the final bits of cooking. Covering food with foil helps too.

- WASH HANDS IMMEDIATELY AFTER HANDLING FRESH CHILLIES!

A COUPLE OF THINGS
THAT WORKED FOR ME

The work tray

I had a tray made out of marine ply, with a deep, vertical rim and beading on the bottom. This way the top can be used for food preparation, and you can flip it over to roll pastry. We are currently trialling different designs of work tray and once we've found the best one the details will be put on my website: https://www. wingingitblind.com

If getting something like this made is not possible, you'll be able to find something suitable in terms of a large tray with sides in a shop or online.

Wire food baskets

There is a film on YouTube showing a blind person using a wire basket in a saucepan to boil eggs. I think this is a brilliant idea, and it could also be extended to boiling vegetables. The use of a basket removes the risk of scalding when you are blind.

I will be investigating this and will put the details of what I find on my website.

WHAT TO DO IF A PAN CATCHES FIRE

- Do not panic.
- Turn the heat off and remove the pan from the heat if safe to do so.
- Wet a clean tea towel in water and drape over the fire to cut off oxygen.
- If it's not safe to remove the pan, wet a clean towel in water and drape over the fire.
- Let everything fully cool down before cleaning up.
- Only open the windows when you are sure the fire is out.
- **DO NOT THROW WATER ON A FAT FIRE!**

Most fires can be controlled in the first minute. Any longer than that, get out, **but do not rush.**

ABOUT THE AUTHOR

Simon Mahoney is a 73-year-old blind veteran. Since losing his sight he has become a passionate advocate for people with sight loss. He is both a member of and a volunteer with Blind Veterans UK, the service charity for servicemen and veterans with sight loss.

He finds the notion of a 'blind community' quite appalling. He feels that just because you cannot see there is no reason to stop being regarded as a real and independent person. He does not have impaired sight, he has none at all. When people ask him how much he can see, his response is to ask what part of blindness do they not get.

He has published one book already – a narrative of his sight loss called *A Descent into Darkness* – and has written numerous articles for health publications. He is currently working on the sequel to his first book called *Winging it Blind*. He is also writing a book about the family for his grandchildren.

His wife died suddenly just before the

Covid-19 pandemic lockdown. Needing to choose between declaring himself helpless and just getting on with looking after himself with no eyes in the house, he chose the latter. The book *First Catch Your Rabbit* is a direct consequence of his accelerated independence.

His ambition is to set up a peer support network for people with sight loss, as he feels that those with sight loss are the real experts.

He continues to live in Derbyshire with his three dogs and a cat called Spitfire.

Please do feel free to get in touch with me at simon@wingingitblind.com and www.wingingitblind.com, where you can find my blog, information about myself and other bits.

●●●

Simon's first book, *Descent into Darkness,* was nominated for the Blind Veterans UK Award for Creativity, and can be found here:

https://www.amazon.co.uk/Descent-Into-Darkness-Simon-Mahoney/dp/1916446302

●●●

Simon's next book, *Winging it Blind*, will be published in 2021, and he is currently working on a second book of recipes, *Rabbit Companion.*

Made in United States
North Haven, CT
23 April 2022

18494822R00157